SACRIFICE at VICKSBURG

Letters from the Front

EDITED BY
Susan T. Puck

Burd Street Press

This Burd Street Press publication
was printed by
Beidel Printing House, Inc.
63 West Burd Street
Shippensburg, PA 17257-0152 USA

In respect for the scholarship contained herein, the acid-free paper used in this book meets the guidelines for permanence and durability of the Committee on Production Guidelines for Book Longevity of the Council on Library Resources.

For a complete list of available publications
please write
Burd Street Press
Division of White Mane Publishing Company, Inc.
P.O. Box 152
Shippensburg, PA 17257-0152 USA

Library of Congress Cataloging-in-Publication Data

Sacrifice at Vicksburg : letters from the front / edited by Susan T. Puck.
p. cm.
Includes bibliographical references (p.) and index.
ISBN 1-57249-047-0 (alk. paper)
1. United States. Army. Wisconsin Infantry Regiment, 23rd (1862–1865) 2. United States--History--Civil War, 1861–1865--Personal narratives. 3. Wisconsin--History--Civil War, 1861–1865--Personal narratives. 4. Soldiers--Wisconsin--Columbia County--Correspondence. 5. Grant, Ulysses S. (Ulysses Simpson), 1822–1885. 6. Vicksburg (Miss.)--History--Siege, 1863--Personal narratives. 7. Richmond family--Correspondence. 8. Columbia County (Wis.)--Biography. I. Puck, Susan T., 1924–
E537.5 23rd.S23 1997
973.7'475--dc21 96-49465
CIP

PRINTED IN THE UNITED STATES OF AMERICA

Table of Contents

List of Illustrations

Introduction

In February 1939, Laurence Palmer Richmond, a 38-year-old electrical engineer, married a widow with two young girls, and my sister and I got our "Pappy," our dear step-father for forty-nine years until his death in 1988. Among his effects were hundreds of letters and papers, some decades old, including some that I knew as the "Civil War letters" but had never read. These were put aside to be transcribed when I had more time.

Five years later, as I was finally transcribing, I began to realize that not only were the letters interesting in themselves but, taken together with what I knew about the family history, they told a coherent story starting with the Civil War and ending fifty years later.

Although I had to do far more historical research than I ever expected to do, this is not intended to be a history book. The historical descriptions are there merely to make the references in the letters more understandable. The letters are the story. They have been transcribed exactly as written, with punctuation and spelling intact. In a few cases I have inserted a name or other clarification in brackets. All of the letters except two were taken directly from the originals. One of the two is from a Lodi, Wisconsin, *Enterprise* of March 10, 1899, and the other is from a very old hand-written copy of the original.

The family history and genealogy were taken from hand-written notes made by my dad and his aunts at various times as well as from existing original documents. The few places where the information was either hearsay or a family story are clearly stated as such. Other sources are detailed in the "Bibliographical Note."

This story is dedicated to all the soldiers of Columbia County, Wisconsin, past and present, and especially to the memory of Colonel Laurence Palmer Richmond, USAF.

1997 Susan T. Puck

The Letter Writers

Three soldiers of Company H, 23rd Regiment, Wisconsin Volunteer Infantry.

Sgt. William Shurtleff, 26, resident of West Point, Columbia County, Wisconsin, wrote to both Mary and Martha Van Ness. Will's sister Clara was married to their brother Walter.

Edgar Richmond, 25, a Company musician, also from West Point, wrote to his sister Adeline and her husband, Isaac Van Ness, brother to Mary, Martha, and Walter.

Thomas Townsend, 23, a farm hand for a West Point farmer, wrote to Martha (Mattie) Van Ness.

The People Back Home

The Peter Van Ness family

Isaac and Adeline Van Ness. Adeline was Edgar Richmond's sister.

Mary Van Ness, 19, sister to Isaac, Mattie, and Walter.

Martha (Mattie) Van Ness, 23, another sister.

Mary, Martha, and Isaac had another brother, Walter, who was married to William Shurtleff's sister Clara.

Other assorted people mentioned in the letters will be identified, where possible, in the text.

1

Wisconsin to Porkopolis

The Civil War was not going at all well for the North in the summer of 1862. Not only had the quick victory the Union had anticipated not materialized, but the Union had suffered humiliating defeats and was about to suffer another one at second Bull Run. There had been few significant victories to compensate.

To the States was given the task of recruitment, and each regiment bore a number and the name of the state where it was formed, i.e., the 96th Ohio or the 6th Massachusetts. Thus it was that many young men, or "boys" as they called themselves, of Columbia County, Wisconsin, enlisted in the 23rd Regiment, Wisconsin Volunteer Infantry, which was mustered into the U.S. service on August 30, 1862. The enlistees of Lodi, a town of about 300 near Madison, and West Point, a farming community near Lodi, became part of Company H of that same regiment. There were so many of them that the company nickname was the "Lodi Badgers."

West Point was a tight-knit community. Most of its farmers had emigrated from New York state in the middle of the previous decade, and some of them still lived in the log cabins their families had built when they first arrived. Indeed, it could be said to be one large family as there had been much intermarriage; not only did the West Point soldiers know each other, they were probably related in some way if only remotely.

Writing was the only way the soldiers and their families could keep in touch, and so a lively correspondence went back and forth from the front, each soldier's letter shared by family members once it was received. The family of Peter Van Ness, a former New Yorker of Dutch ancestry, was the focus of much of this correspondence. Peter had four children, Walter and Isaac, who were grown and married; and Martha (always called Mattie) who was 23 and Mary who was 19.

Three soldiers wrote regularly to this family.

Edgar Richmond was 25 and had been a farmer. His sister Adeline, seven years older, was married to Isaac Van Ness, and their little boy was named for his Uncle Walter. With two exceptions Edgar's letters are all addressed to "Dear Sister and Brother" or "Dear Sister."

William Shurtleff was 26. His sister Clara was married to Walter Van Ness, so Will was well acquainted with the family, but all his letters are written to either Mary or Mattie.

The third soldier, **Thomas Townsend**, 24, was, in a way, an outsider. He was not a long time West Point resident, but it is possible he was distantly related to the Richmonds through a cousin of Edgar Richmond's grandfather who had married a man named George Townsend. Thomas had worked for a local farmer named Milton Bartholomew, knew the young men of the community, and had enlisted with them. All of his letters are addressed to Mattie, in whom he had more than a passing interest. Thomas's sister Sarah lived in Buffalo, New York, but had visited him in West Point, knew the Van Ness sisters, and continued to correspond with Mattie as well as with Edward Streater, another West Point soldier.

Edward Streater had come from New York also. By the time he enlisted he was an orphan. Since he was under twenty-one, he had to bring a certificate from a notary to the enlistment office stating that he was at least 18 and had no parents to give permission for his enlistment.

In the following letter Thomas also mentions "Jimmy" and "Mr. Reed." Jimmy was James Richmond, 21, the son of Edgar's Uncle Simeon, who had died in 1852. James had come to Wisconsin after his mother's remarriage in 1859. Mr. Reed was Russel Reed, related to Mary and Mattie through their mother, who was Emma Reed before her marriage to Peter Van Ness.

The new recruits were sent first to Camp Randall, near Madison, and were close enough that the people of Lodi and West Point could visit them on Sundays.

THOMAS TOWNSEND TO MATTIE VAN NESS:

Camp Randal Friday Sept 5th 62

Dear Friend

I did not recieve your ever useful and most Welcome Gift until it was to late to return my thanks by Note by the bearers So Accept them now and believe me I shall ever remember you in gratitude for your kindness. You say be of good cheer. I try so to be but still when I think of the many dear Friends I have left behind me it makes me feel rather despondent at times but still I feel as though I was doing my duty and shall try and persevere and overcome some of my weaknesses. I have been complaining with sickness considerable since I have been in camp but thank an all wise providence I am feeling a great deal better now. Our Diet is coarse but plenty. I think it was to much of a change it was very different from what I had been used to at any rate, I am sorry that we are to be Hurried of so soon. I expected to get a furlough and come back and stay a few days but I do not see any chance now. I was quite disappointed at not seeing your pleasant face amongst the company from your Home but I suppose we are doomed to disappointment and sorrow in this World. It is raining very fast here this afternoon and it is coming through on the roof into Edwards [Streater] and my bunk if it keeps on much longer we shall have a damp place to sleep to Night. I think it is nothing but right that the Volunteers should be remembered by there Friends at home for no one but those that have tried it know what they have to put up with. Milton and his two oldest daughters were here last Wensday it seemed almost like parting from my Father to part with Milton the girls also were very Friendly the eldest more so than usual. We have some rough boys here but we have a plan of getting along with them very well and that is to let them alone and keep away from them as much as possible. I like our Officers very well they are strict and bound to maintain good order if Possible and that is what we want.

Have you heard from Sarah yet I have not and I begin to feel quite uneasy about her it has quit raining and I must close for we should be called out to drill in a few minutes and must prepare for it. Give my best respects to your Father and Mother also to Mary and Jimmy accept my best wishes yourself and believe me to remain affectionately yours

Thomas Townsend

PS

Please hand the enclosed to Mr Reed and oblige your Friend T Townsend

Write soon if we do not leave here and address

Camp Randall Madison
Dane County
Company H 23 Reg Wis Vol

The men were barely settled at Camp Randall when they were sent off on September 15, with little or no training, to the defense of Cincinnati and attached to the 2nd Brigade, 2nd Division, Army of Kentucky, under the overall command of General Carlos Buell. Confederate Generals E. Kirby Smith and Braxton Bragg were making inroads into Kentucky, and Smith was threatening both Louisville and Cincinnati, then a city of about 200,000. The capture of Cincinnati would have been a real blow to the Union, as the city, "the Queen of the West," was not only important as an access to the Mississippi and as a commercial hub but was "hog butcher for the world" before Chicago out-butchered her. This last activity had earned Cincinnati the common nickname of "Porkopolis."

General Lew Wallace was in charge of the defense of Cincinnati and had not only declared martial law, but had put the civilians to work building the defenses of the city. Most of these defenses were on the Kentucky side of the Ohio River. General Wallace is now better known as the author of the novel, *Ben Hur.*

When Thomas says "We had a rather hard time coming here on the Cars," he means they traveled by rail.

THOMAS TO MATTIE:

Sept 17th/62

I am just going to send you a line to let you know that we arrived safe in Cincinnati this morning and we are now awaiting orders to march to Camp. We had rather a hard time coming here on the Cars for we were kept on about half rations most of the time.

The boys are all in first rate spirits and trying to enjoy themselves to the best of there abilities. The City is under martial law and they have stoped the Sale of all kind of intoxication liquors which I think is a first rate arrangement.

Farewell we have to march best respects to all inquiring Friends and accept my best wishes yourself. From affectionate Friend *Thomas Townsend*

Address Thomas Townsend

Cincinnati Ohio (note indicating this to follow Reg)

I shall write again as soon as possible after we get to camp Farewell yours

Thomas
Co H 23 Reg Wis Vol

Edgar Richmond is listed on the company roll as a musician; his instrument was the fife. In civilian life, besides farming, he played with other musicians for dances. His handwritten music book has the fife part for waltzes, hornpipes, schottisches, and cotillions.

Drummers and fifers were standard company members, and drum majors and fife majors were non-commissioned officers.

Ed Richmond had an adventurous streak which had lead him, in 1859, to join a wagon train to California. Family legend has it that he made it as far as Colorado where he was robbed of his money by one of his fellow travelers. At any rate, he was back in Wisconsin in time to enlist. In speaking of California, he is supposed to have said that it was the only place he knew of where a man didn't have to work hard all summer just to keep warm all winter.

"Ans" was Ansen Burlingame. There were at least six Burlingame families in the Lodi area at this time. Ed Richmond's brother, Dave, was married to Maria Louisa Burlingame.

It is difficult to imagine now the extent of the prejudice and ethnocentrism that existed in the United States in the middle of the nineteenth century. Even the most ardent Abolitionist did not necessarily believe that the Negro was the equal of the white man, just that slavery was evil. The prejudice was not just against people of a different race. There was a kind of hierarchy of discrimination with the slave at the bottom. The Irish were discriminated against in New York where job openings advertised "No Irish need apply," and in Wisconsin there was a definite, if more subtle, discrimination against the Norwegians.

During the years before the Civil War, Wisconsin had very few, if any, black residents. Even at the time of the 1870 census there was only one black in the Lodi-West Point area. Thus it is not surprising that the Wisconsin soldiers talked about the slaves in a manner that would not be tolerated by thinking people today.

Ed Richmond's letters are considerably more outspoken than those of the other men, probably because he was writing to his older sister and brother-in-law instead of to a lady friend and so did not have to follow the accepted conventions a gentleman was supposed to observe when writing to a young lady.

ED RICHMOND TO ADELINE AND WALTER VAN NESS:

In camp up the Ohio river 4 miles from Cincinnati Sept 19th 1862

Dear Brother & Sister we are now encamped on the border of the enemies country, & I tell you things begin to look a little like war. There is reported to be 100,000 troops within 60 miles of this vicinity. I have no doubt of it, the Ohio river is fortified for many miles on the Kentucky side, of course. The rebels are 15 miles from here now, although they have been some little skirmishing and a few prisoners taken a day or two before we got here. The probability is now that we will not have a fight here. 4 brigades left here yesterday for some place farther down the river among them was the 11th Wis Reg. I didnt get a chance to see any of the boys one fellow of our company Bill Wheeler said he saw 3 of them. We are on the left wing of the army under General Wallace. Now as to the description of the country. I can say it is the roughest I ever was in there is nothing else but hills and mountain, yet there is considerable corn raised here & I tell you Ike it is big. I did not believe Gil when he used to say that they rode through their corn horse back to husk it in Ill. but I believe they will have to do it here or chop it down. I paced a stalk yesterday & it was 13 feet high it was 6 feet to the butt of the ear, but the average of the corn is 12 feet

Grapes are cultivated quite extensively - every farmer has several acres the grapes have been gathered so we dont get any. Peaches are raised in abundance. We are now encamped in a peach orchard but like the grapes they are all picked. The Apple trees are large & remind me of eastern orchards. there is several orchard in sight but darn the Sentinels we cant get out I have not seen many nigger yet & what I have seen was using the spade pick or axe. The captain took us down to the river to go in swiming last night. the home guard gun boat was going down the river. it runs up & down the river for about 60 miles it is a kind of tellegraph. I believe the boys are all well at present & appear to be in good spirits most of them are writing letters. I guess you would laugh if you could see me setting up beside a peach tree a writing on my knee, but this only one of the thousand positions that you might see.

We have not got all our tents yet but are to have them to day. The boys will be glad for we had to sleep in the open air the last 2 night. I must tell you about the boys that was on guard last night. The grand rounds went round to see how many guns he could get away from the boys & he got every gun but 3 from the second relief. Ans [Ansen Burlingame] said he tried to get his but by G-d he didnt do it the boys will learn something after a little.

We have had pretty hard fare for a day or two but I think we will have better now we have got settled. We had ham coffee & sugar hard crackers for breakfast that is good enough but I am going to tell you what we had yesterday & day before. We had meat and bread that had been packed 3 days before we started from camp Randall the bread was mouldy & sour & the meat had maggots in it an inch long. We had to put a guard of 6 over it to keep it from running off. hip hip who wouldnt be a soldier. well I dont find any fault - it is just as I expected.

I must draw to a close & go and see the boys shoot at a target. now Ike write soon & tell me how all the folks get along you & Adeline together can write a good long letter

I shall write to someone in West Point every day or two for a while so you will hear from me

E X Richmond

P.S. Direct to E——R—— Cincinnati Ohio

Company H. 23 Reg Wis Vol
if you direct in this way the letters will be forwarded to us

---

Wisconsin was admitted to the Union as the thirtieth state in 1848, and the University of Wisconsin was founded that same year. By the time of the Civil War, there were at least six colleges in the state, showing the importance that education had for the settlers.

Even though the Van Ness sisters were essentially country girls, they were well educated and read a lot. Their early lives were spent in a home near the farm made famous in "The Legend of Sleepy Hollow," and according to family history, they knew Washington Irving, who was still living when they left New York. As they were in their teens when they came to Wisconsin, their early education was in New York schools.

The women were intelligent and had wide-ranging interests, especially in plants and flowers. Mary was noted in Lodi all her life for her garden.

Although in none of his letters does he give his address or rank, Will Shurtleff was actually a sergeant, one of five in the company. Easily the most learned of the men, he had given Mary a small book as a present just as the company left Camp Randall. It was *The Songs and Ballads of Sir Walter Scott*, handsomely bound in tooled leather with gilt edges on the pages. On the fly leaf was written in pencil, "To Mary from Will," and in the upper right corner of the same page, "Sept. 8, 1862."

Sergeant William T. Shurtleff
Photograph courtesy of James P. Schmiedlin, Lodi, Wisconsin

Gib was Gilbert Reynolds, a friend of all three men and the son of Sylvester Reynolds, a prominent citizen of Lodi.

Will Shurtleff to Mary Van Ness:

Camp Bates Kentucky Sept 25 [1862]

Dear Mary

I will now try to redeem my promise to write to my friends as often as possible but I must say that we have much less leisure than I expected. We are so green in military affairs that we are obliged to improve the most of our time in learning our new business. The Colonel is strict to the letter of military law but he is well liked by the regiment. Besides the regular drill he gets us together every day or two and gives us a lesson or lecture. Sunday our lesson was on the duty of sentinals in camp—yesterday on picket guards and patrols, and by the way, I was out on picket duty 24 hours, from Monday till Tuesday morning. We went about three miles from camp and enjoyed ourselves pretty well under the circumstances. No rebels were in sight or hearing so far as we know and probably none within forty miles. This part of the state is very rough and mostly cultivated in fruit and truck for the Cincinnati market. Our lines of guards and pickets must be a source of constant vexation to the market people on this side of the river and besides this, the fields for miles around are cut up with rifle pits and fortifications, but these are only some of the minor blessings of the rebellion. We don't know much about the positions of our army south of Cincinnati but if you take a map and describe a semi circle commencing seven or eight miles above on the river and ending the same distance below and scatter an indefinite number of regiments and batteries in a very indefinite manner over the ground you will have as good an idea of it as I have. At present the vicinity of Louisville is supposed to be the theater of active operations. The most of our boys are well and hearty although we have lived out of doors ever since coming to Kentucky. This afternoon they are building little tents with their blankets. Bancroft was sent to the hospital a day or two ago sick with a fever but now I hear he is better. Robt Maynard went there this morning with sore eyes. Lockwood of Lodi has been appointed Hospital Warden—a pretty good place with $20.50 per month.

From what I heard the Colonel say I think we may leave this place pretty soon but letters will come straight if directed to Cincinnati.

I have some leaves of geranium and myrtle in my memorandum book that I intend to keep till I go back to West Point. I shall expect that you have already written to me and I'll look for a letter by Saturday night at farthest.

From Your Friend
Will

Gib says "tell Walt I'll write to him in a day or two"

In the following letter Will Shurtleff says, "When you see that school ma'm, tell her that I have forgotten how to make a night- cap." Exactly what kind he was talking about was not clear. It may have been the cloth kind that kept the head warm since fall and cold weather were coming on. It was most assuredly not a drink which contained hard liquor. Most of the good farmers of West Point were strongly against "demon rum," and any school ma'm who advocated putting liquor in a drink would quickly find herself out of a job.

The "certain young gentleman" Will mentions may have been Thomas, in which case Will was teasing Mattie a bit.

WILLIAM TO MATTIE:

Camp Bates Sept 29th [1862]

Dear Mattie

I don't know whether I promised positively to write or not but as I have a little leisure just now I'll do it with pleasure, believing that you will not hesitate to answer my letter soon. If you should be afraid of offending a certain young gentleman thereby, I think you might make a satisfactory explanation to him at the same time—any way so that I get a letter. One reason why I have leisure is that we have received our tents to-day and I can write by candle light until "taps". I have had no letters from home yet, and it seems a long time since I heard from West Point—perhaps I'm getting homesick- "Therefore I say unto you all write".

The talk is that we may leave this place soon. I merely give the rumor for what it is worth as we have had no orders from head quarters. The surgeon is sending the sick to the general hospital—Bancroft is among them The quartermaster too, surmises that we may soon have a forward movement and is arranging his department accordingly. On the other hand they are still building rifle pits etc. as though we were to wait for an attack. Perhaps this may be merely to guard against possible surprise.

We have now just five tents to each company viz one small wall tent for the commissioned officers, one ditto for five sergeants and a company clerk and three bell tents for the privates. This is stowing the boys in pretty close - from 24 to 29 in a tent. If you see that school ma'm, tell her that I have forgotten how to make a night-cap. I would like to see some of you and take lessons once again. I've tried it two or three times and didn't succeed. Well I didn't have time to finish any letter last night and now we are just in from forenoon drill. I have not attempted to write a single letter but that I have been interrupted, sometimes more than once. This is a good school for an irritable or nervous man to learn patience and kindred virtues. The tent is getting so full now that it is almost impossible to write so I'll say good bye for a little while and expect a letter from you soon.

From Your friend
W.T. Shurtleff

Although "hard cracker" sounds rather unappetizing, the cracker, also called hardtack, was part of the standard rations for the Union army. Made of flour and water, it was approximately three inches by three inches and a half inch thick.[1] When made correctly, it could be crumbled and was usually eaten crumbled in coffee. However, it was not always made correctly, being sometimes moldy, sometimes too hard to break, and frequently weevil infested. A day's marching rations consisted of a pound (either nine or ten) of these crackers, three-quarters of a pound of meat when available, coffee, and sugar.

A bell tent was eighteen feet in diameter, twelve feet high in the middle, and shaped like a tepee. Since it was said to be comfortable for a dozen men, 24 to 29 in each must have been quite cramped. The men slept in a bell tent like the spokes of a wheel with their heads at the rim and their feet at the hub. The preferred position was directly opposite the door as this place was the safest from being stepped on by latecomers.[2]

Will had previously written that Bancroft was in the hospital, meaning the field hospital which was attached to the regiment. In this letter he said that the surgeon was sending the sick to the general hospital—Bancroft among them. The general hospitals were established stationary hospitals where the men were sent when they were well enough to travel but needed a long recovery time. The conditions at the general hospital, while not good, were considerably better than the field hospitals, which were frequently tents with beds of straw on the ground for the patients.

Will said that Lockwood of Lodi was appointed Hospital Warden at $20.50 a month. Since a private in the Union Army received $13.00 a month, Lockwood, indeed, had "a pretty good place."

THOMAS TO MATTIE:

Camp Bates Kentucky Oct 5th 62

Dear Mattie

I will own to you that I am a little disappointed at not receiving a letter from you ere this but shall not pretend to scold you, for you know of course that the men folks dont know how to do any such thing. I presume you think is strange that I do not write you. It is just in this way. I wrote you a short note from Porkopolis all I had time to write and I thought I would wait a few days and get an answer from that and then write to you again but as I have not got any from you I shall write again. We were very pleasantly situated in a Peach Orchard till this Morning but this Morning we struck our tents and moved about A Mile to take charge of a Fort. We are now about six miles from Cincinnati and a mile from the Ohio River. The Regiment has just gone out on dress parade but I did not feel well so I did not go. It is the first time I have felt unwell since I have been In Kentucky. I hope I shall feel better in the Morning. The rest of the boys that you are accuainted with are all well. We are getting along with our drill very well. We have had quite a number of Puffs since we have been here. We are called the best Reg that ever came in to Kentucky. That is saying considerable. I recd a letter from Sarah a day or two ago she said she had not recd any from you also said that I was to scold you for not writing to her but I dont think I shall for I am not in a scolding mood to Night. Our Board is considerable better that it was we have good light Bread now in the place of Hard Crackers.

Monday Morn

I had to give up my writing last Night on account of Headache and noise in the tent and it is not much better this morning for A Burlingame is using some pretty strong terms in regard to the Cooks. I think some time if it was not for Anson we should not have any noise at all. The report has been current here lately that we were to March to Lexington but I think that we shall slip up on that for it looks as though we were going to stay here some time if not Longer. I will now try and give you a list of the boys that are in the tent that I am in B Waffle H, to [Byron and Harevy Waffle] G. Reynolds G Kingsley J M Bartholomew G Phinney C Passage E Riddle JC Brown E Streater A Burlingame and T Townsend

There are seventeen of us altogether but I believe that is all you know of them. We have all pledged ourselves not to play cards so long as the War Continues and to use all our influence against it with those in our tent that have been in the Habit of playing.

I will now try and give you a little description of the Country. It is very Rough Hilly and broken, Small steep hills with very deep Ravines between. the Soil is a kind of Clay looks very poor and does not belie its looks at all it is a first rate fruit Country they raise nice peaches and grapes. There apples are not of the best variety but they are plenty. It is not as much pleasure for us to brush up and fix ourselves as it was in Camp Randall for there are but very few Ladys that come out to see us here And if they are a fair Sample of Southern Ladys it is my candid Opinion That Wisconsin will take the lead so far as beauty with the Fair Sex is Concerned. I have been out on Picket once since I have been here but I did not have the Pleasure of Seeing any Rebels but The Night after I was out an Ohio Reg brought in three prisoners but I have not seen them. I like Picketing very well for we can get some apples and cider and many other things that we cant get in camp. Guard is rather dull it is so much the same thing over and over again. I get some what lonesome Nights on guard and think of old times past and gone and hope We may all return safe and sound to enjoy ourselves amongst our Friends again. I have just heard the name of the Fort we are garrisoning it is Fort Whittlesey. I have not seen the inside of it yet yet for we cant get around without a pass and our Captain has not had time to write any yet. Now Mattie I would like to recieve a letter from you as soon as you like to write for I Tell you a good letter makes us feel almost as though we were at home. I would give a dollar for a letter from you just at this present time so write soon. I have not heard from Milton yet and he promise faithfully to write me as soon as he recd one from me and I wrote him as soon as I got here.

Give my best respects to Russel and Family and tell them I shall be happy to hear from them as soon as they can make it convenient to write. With best respects to your own Family and Love to yourself

I remain truly Your
Friend T Townsend

Please Direct

Cincinnati Ohio
Co H 23 Reg
Wis Vol

Please excuse my many mistakes for there is such a noise and my head aches so I can hardly see the lines

Farewell Mattie
be a good girl

Up to this point Thomas has signed himself "affectionately yours," or "affectionate friend," but here he has become bold and sent Mattie "Love to yourself." This was rather daring on his part, as he ran a very real danger of being upbraided for taking unwelcome liberties with her. He might have embarrassed her, too, as most letters were circulated among family and friends. There is no record of what Mattie may or may not have said, but after two more letters with a salutation of "Dear Mattie" and "Love" in closing, he goes back to the more formal "Dear Friend" or "Friend Mattie," and never again says "Dear Mattie" or sends her his love or affection, only his regards.

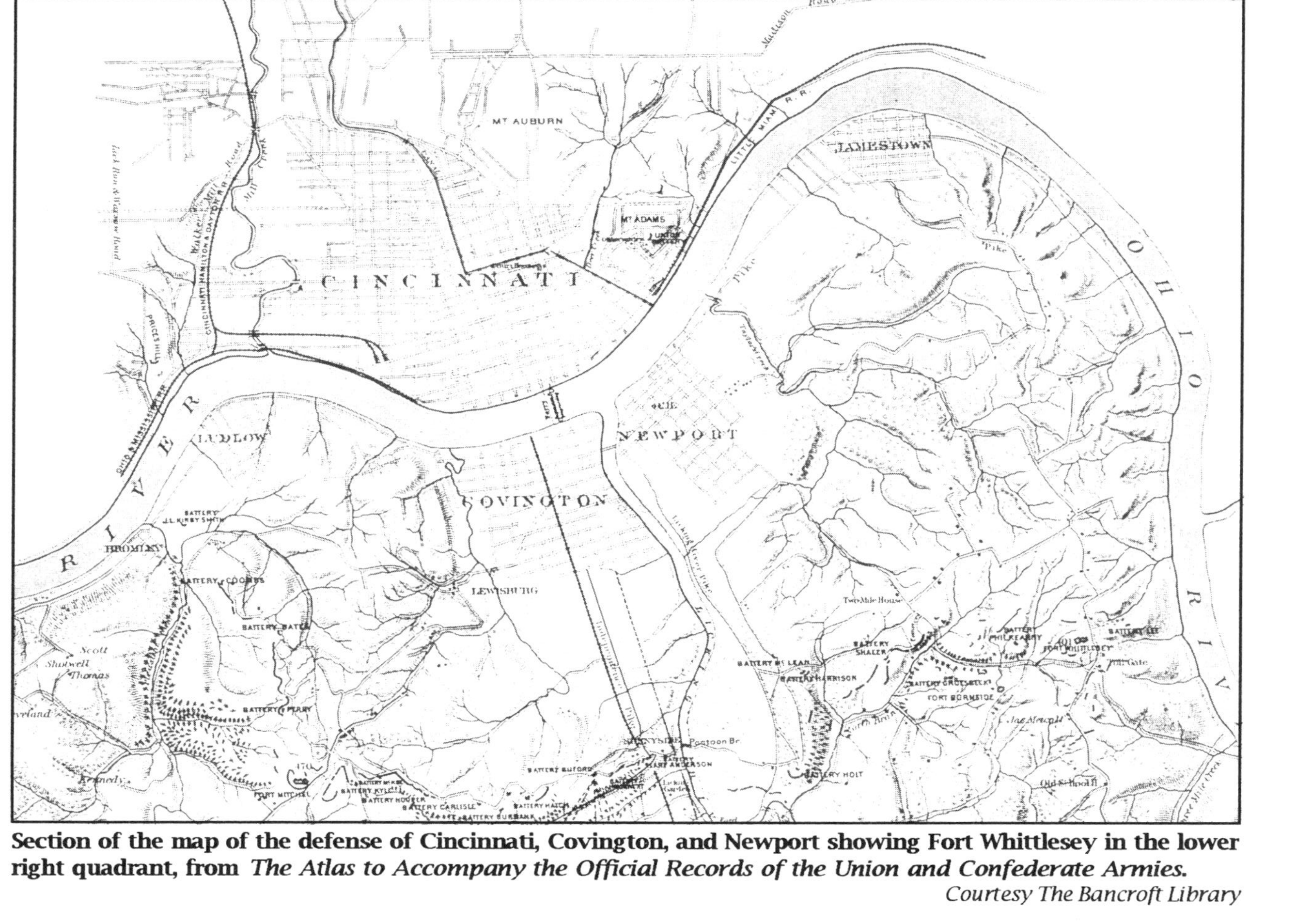

Section of the map of the defense of Cincinnati, Covington, and Newport showing Fort Whittlesey in the lower right quadrant, from *The Atlas to Accompany the Official Records of the Union and Confederate Armies.*

Courtesy The Bancroft Library

UNION! [n.d.]

I am sorry that the young folks should all be offended at you but still I dont think it is worth your slightest notice You wished me to send you some wild Flowers could I find them I have not seen a wild flower worthy of Notice since I have been in kentucky If they call this the sunny South where they have so many pretty Flowers I would seek mine at the North rather than the South We are having very fine Weather here at present Although it is very warm during the day The dust is blowing here to day awful these sheets of paper will not be fit to send by the time I get through

Letter from Thomas Townsend
Kentucky, [October] 1862

Private collection of Susan T. Puck

In the following letter Thomas refers to Ed as a "little boy." Since Ed, at five feet, six and a half inches, was only an inch and a half shorter than Thomas at five feet, eight inches, the reference must be to their respective weights.

THOMAS TO MATTIE:

Date unk [Kentucky 62]

first part missing

I am Sorry that the young folks should all be offended at you but still I dont think it is worth your slightest notice. You wished me to send you some wild Flowers could I find them. I have not seen a wild flower worthy of Notice since I have been in Kentucky. If they call this the sunny South where they have so many pretty Flowers I would seek mine at the North rather than the South. We are having very fine Weather here at present Although it is very warm during the day. The dust is blowing here to day awful these sheets of paper will not be fit to send by the time I get through.

I will now try and give you a little description of things we get up for fun and excitement. Last Night we made an Elephant by having Four of us Boys stooping over and covered up with blankets then all move at together and make as horrid a noise as possible another performance is for a little fellow to get on a large mans shoulders and a still smaller one to get up on the second ones shoulders and have a large blanket or two over there head and then they travel of looking like a tree or something of that sort. The performance winding up with running a foot race getting of long yarns or singing songs. Mary wishes to know how I like the southern girls. I like them very well so far as I know anything about them. I think they are pretty good kind of girls they dont say any thing to me so of course I dont say any thing to them. I have seen but very few pretty girls not half so many as I left behind me when I left Wisconsin.

E Richmond is lying in the tent along side of me he is getting so fat and lazy he cant hardly move he says he has gained 14 pounds since leaving Camp Randall pretty well for a little boy like him is it not

Give my best respects to Juliette B, if you please and any other that may enquire for me. With kind wishes for Mary and Love for yourself believe me to remain truly your Friend *Thomas*

Direct the same as before and oblige
yours in haste Thomas

In his 1861 inauguration speech, Lincoln had said,

"I have no purpose, directly or indirectly, to interfere with the institution of slavery in the states where it exists. I believe I have no lawful right to do so, and I have no inclination to do so."

However, by the summer of 1862 he was under great pressure to free the slaves by members of his own party, and the argument threatened to split the Republicans. In July he brought an Emancipation Proclamation to his cabinet but was persuaded to delay issuing it until the Union had won a real victory in battle. While the battle at Antietam was not as complete a victory as he had hoped, it was enough to bring out the proclamation again. In it Lincoln said that the states which returned to the Union within one hundred days would be compensated for their slaves; those who did not would lose their slaves without compensation when the Union won the war. On September 23, he gave this proclamation to the public, but it was not officially signed until January 1, 1863.

An "on dit" (literally "one says") is a bit of gossip.

WILL TO MARY:

Fort Whittlesey, Oct 7th [1862]

Friend Mary

I received your note of the 28th last evening and you can guess it was very welcome. Our letters are so long on the road that it seems as though they were never coming. I wrote to you a few days since but I can't recollect now just when it was of what I wrote so if I should happen to make recapitulations you will at least for this once excuse me.

We packed up our traps and left Camp Bates on Sunday morning (it was wicked perhaps, but according to orders) and came to this place which is about half a mile from the old camp. This fort consists of two large square enclosures surrounded by a high earthwork wall and a deep ditch on the outside. Our left rests on the fort and the right is protected by rifle pits. We are on high ground and from where we are we can see the camp of the 96th Ohio about a mile to our right and similarly protected by rifle pits and a heavy battery. We are resting here in a very pleasant uncertainty about what we are to do. I think the Colonel is ready and willing to go into active service just as soon as the powers that be will give him permission.

There is a little *on dit* in camp concerning our late review. As the 23d moved past the reviewing officer and staff Gen Wright, commander of department observed "There is a splendid regiment.

They should be started south immediately." To which Smith our Division General replied that if his best troops were to be taken from him he would resign. This is what Madam Rumor gives as the reason of our protracted stay near Cincinnati.

You speak of the Emancipation proclamation of the President and ask my views. I have no hesitation in saying that I believe him right. Years ago Jefferson advocated the emancipation of the blacks. Good men and true believed and hoped that it might be gradually and peacefully effected. But southern slavocrats have blindly and madly attempted to set up an empire on the ruins of our old republic with slavery for its foundation stone. With our views of right and wrong this is impossible for although we might tolerate slavery while there was a prospect of its ultimate abolition we can not uphold it when it attempts to override every other interest. No doubt all would be glad to have the question peacefully settled. The south now has the privelege of returning to the old union with all the rights heretofore enjoyed but if her usurping rulers hesitate they will inaugurate an era of the freedom of all races a freedom baptized perhaps in the best blood of the nation but if it is to be a step forward in the worlds progress we can but say amen.

We are not far enough south to know whether the proclamation will have any effect beyond the lines of our armies or not. There are but few slaves in this section and I presume they are well treated otherwise they could crop the Ohio with very little trouble "Uncle Tom's Cabin" to the contrary notwithstanding

Ed sends his "respects". Write soon to

Your friend
W.T. Shurtleff

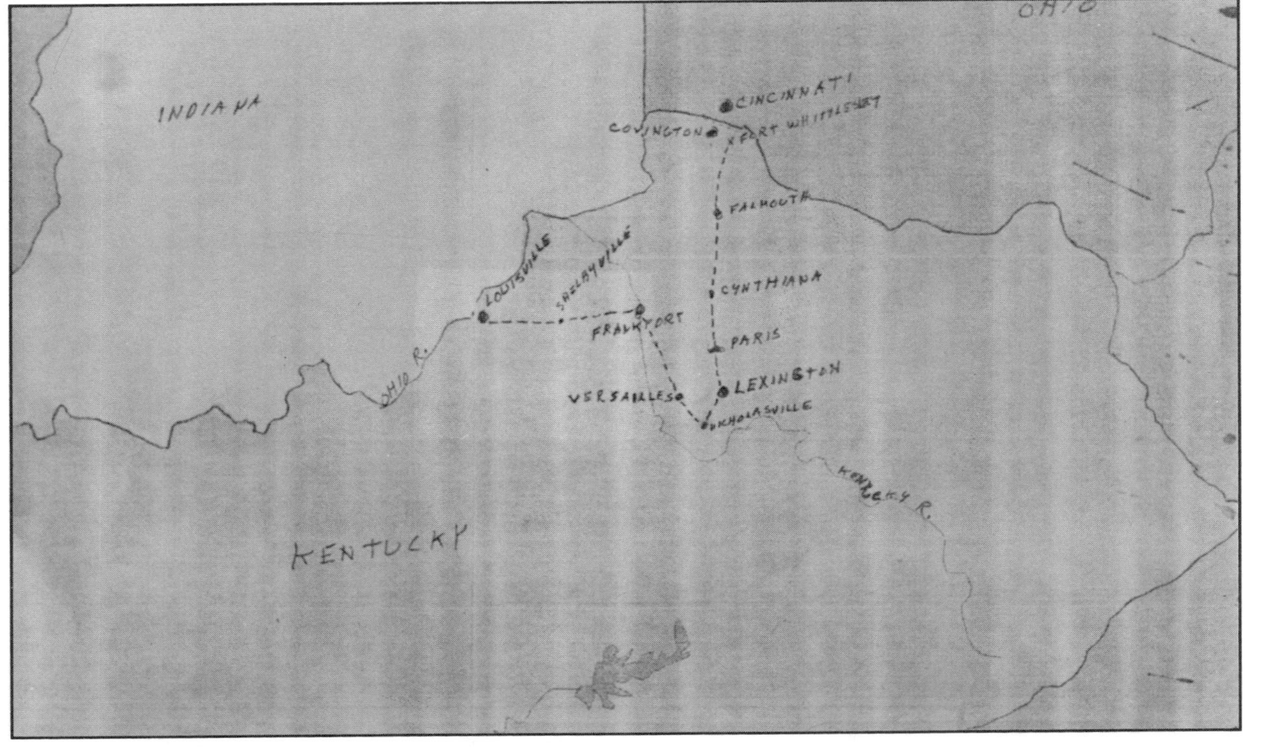

Route followed by 23rd Wisconsin Infantry, Cincinnati, Ohio to Louisville, Kentucky, the long way. October 8 – November 15, 1863

Map by editor

2

Cincinnati to Louisville the Long Way

During the summer and fall of 1862, Kentucky suffered from a severe drought, and all the armies there had difficulty getting water since they depended on springs and streams for their supply.[3]

Members of the Confederate Army were referred to as "Rebels," and the "Secesh" (short for secession) were the people of the states that had seceded. The Confederate soldiers were sometimes called "Butternuts" as many of them wore homemade uniforms dyed with a stain made from butternut or walnut hulls, a sort of yellowish-brown.

Thomas to Mattie:

Oct 12th 62
Falmouth Kentucky

Dear Mattie

I thought I would write you another letter to let you know that we had changed our Residence. We left Camp Bates last Wenesday morning With our Knapsacks strapped on our backs for what place we knew not. We marched very nearly all day and were very tired when Night came. The next Morning we started again. That day we got ahead of our baggage train and just before Night we crossed a creek or rather the bed of a creek for it is dry now. We had a very steep hill to go down to it and still steeper to get up again and by that we gained still more on the teams we camped that Night just up on the hill. Our team did not come to the Creek till after dark and that Morning we had put all our Knapsacks on the Wagon so that we had to wait till they came before we could lay down to sleep. The most of us went down the hill again to get our Knapsacks and of all the whipping and swearing I never heard anything to equal that Nights Noise. The Officers calling the Wagons rattling on the stones and the Mules neighing made delightful music. We got our Knapsacks about eleven oclock and were up again the next morning at three and were very soon on the road. That day we stopped about Noon and put up our tents for it looked very much like rain. That Night I was on Picket and got into Camp in the morning just as the Regiment was Ready to March and fell in with them and marched to were we are now. Here we expect to stay some time a week at least and probaly longer. Ever Since we started from Camp Bates we have been kept on half Rations and have had the hardest kind of work to get water to drink. This is the most miserable country for water I ever saw. We are now in Secesh Country. The Cavalry were out yesterday and brought in quite a number of prisoners. Some of our troops took sixty good Beef Cattle yesterday from a Secesh that was Droving for the Rebel army So that Respect we shall have Enough meat for some time now. We are confiscating considerable now And I hope we shall continue to do so. We are in General Smiths Brigade and they are all here with us and part of another Brigade there is between eight and ten thousand of us here including Cavalry and Artillery. It is quite a pretty sight to look over our Camp and see all the tents especially in the evening when they are all light up. We are going to have quite a treat for Supper to Night almost all the boys in our tent have been down to the River this afternoon and got a large pot full of Clams and we are going to have a stew.

An Ohio Reg that was with us took a Rebel the second day we were on the March and when he found he was trapped he ran against a tree and tried to knock his brains out but he did not succeed although he gave our Surgeon quite a little job to sew up his wounds. They have been bringing in prisoners at intervals all day. We have not seen them but we hear some of our boys cheering like good fellows whenever they bring them in they say that Bragg is all cut to pieces and his Army scattered they think that we shall not have any fighting to do in Kentucky how that is I will not pretend to say

We are now about Forty miles South East of. Porkopolis near a town called Falmouth. The Rebels were here only a week ago. They had a little fight here eight Union men fought against thirty five Rebels and killed eleven and drove the others. But before they left they burnt some buildings and a large Railroad Bridge the Bridge I believe we have to build again. The Boys in our tent say that whenever we write to a young Lady we must give her the Respects of the whole tent so I will send them to you. We have had our supper

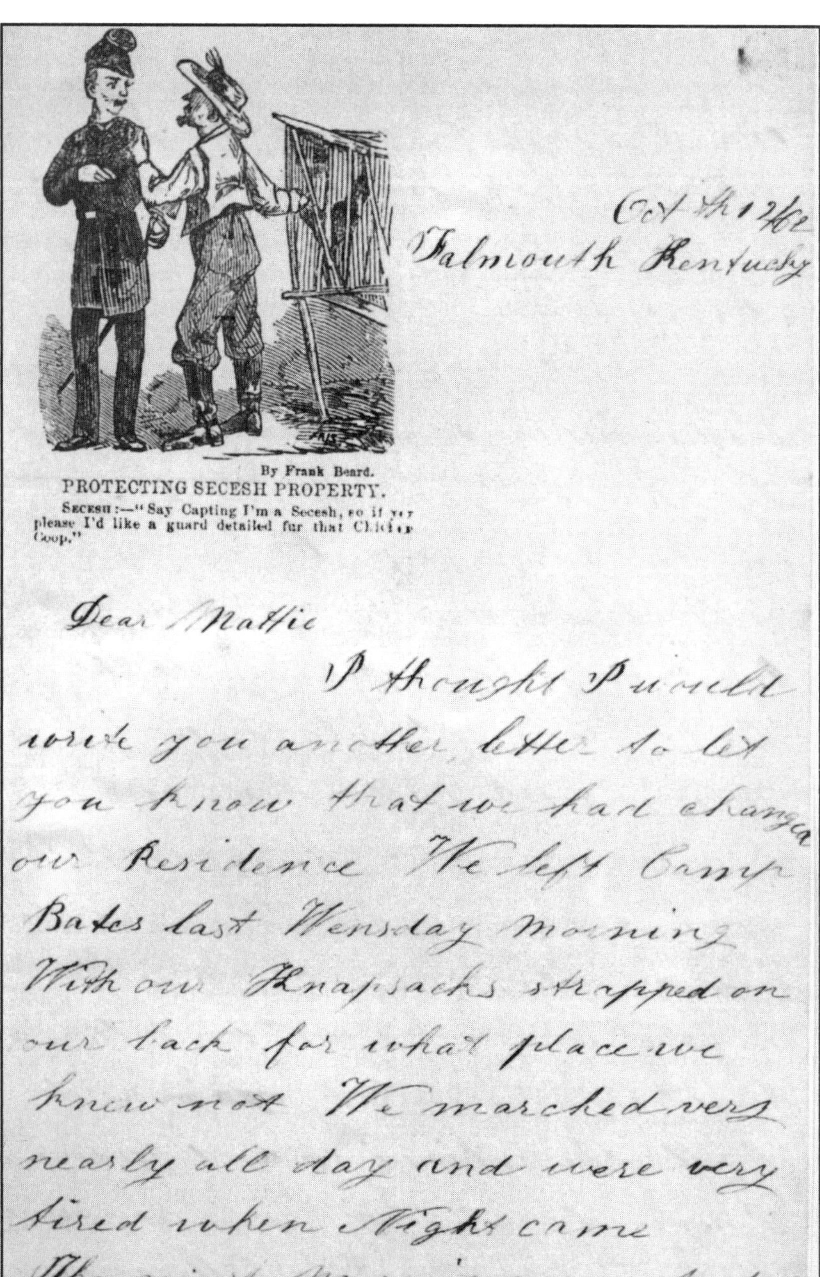

By Frank Beard.

PROTECTING SECESH PROPERTY.

SECESH:—"Say Capting I'm a Secesh, so if yer please I'd like a guard detailed fur that Chicken Coop."

Oct the 12/62
Falmouth Kentucky

Dear Mattie

I thought I would write you another letter to let you know that we had changed our Residence We left Camp Bates last Wensday Morning With our Knapsacks strapped on our back for what place we knew not We marched very nearly all day and were very tired when Night came The nisct Morning we started again Thrt day we got ahead of

Letter from Thomas Townsend
October 12, 1862
Private collection of Susan T. Puck

enjoyed our Clam soup very well had some nice apple sauce to that also went first rate.

Monday morning

It looks rather dismal here this morning it is quite cloudy and a kind of drizzling rain falling it begins to look like real fall Weather here now. I shall have to bring this to a close for I have to write to Sarah this morning. Give my respects to Mary and all other enquiring Friends if any there be. Accept my Love yourself and believe me to remain truly yours

Thomas Townsend

Please Direct

Company H 23 Reg
Wis Vol
Second Brigade
Second Division
Second Army Corps
Department of Ohio
Via Cincinnati

If you dont think this will be Directions enough to bring the letter here please put on a little more. Farewell Mattie

Excuse this dirty paper and poor writing for it is the best I could do this time for I am running behind with my writing.

Good Bye

Contrary to Thomas's information, Bragg's army was not "all cut to pieces," but was withdrawing after a battle at Perryville, Kentucky, on October 8. Neither side could claim a victory, but Bragg's information about the size of Buell's army was such that he deemed it prudent to withdraw, much to the dismay of some of his subordinates, especially E. Kirby Smith.[4]

About this time the 23rd Regiment was attached to the 1st Brigade, 1st Division of the Army of Kentucky.

The route the regiment was following was along the Licking River, the source of the dinner clams. The Kentucky Central Railroad also followed this route to Falmouth.

In the following letter to his sister Adeline, Ed Richmond mentions Mary, George, Dave, and Sarah, who were his other brothers and sisters. Of these, only Sarah was younger than Ed.

EDGAR RICHMOND TO ADELINE VAN NESS:

Camp near Falmouth Ky
Oct 14th 1862

Dear Sister

Again I seat myself to write a few lines to you. I have received no answer to the letters I have written to yet. the reason I cant account for neither have I received any from Dave or George. I wrote Sarah & Mary after I did to you & have received a prompt answer but as we have altered our camping place & been on the march for 4 days, I will write a gain & tell you a little about the proceedings. In the morning at 4 oclock Oct 8th we were waked out of a deep slumber & ordered to get ready for a march we packed knapsacks drawed 2 days rations or what had to answer for the same (it realy was not enough for one day) Struck tents & was ready to march a little after sunrise. The sun shone very warm. we had our knapsacks to carry & we had a pretty hard time of it although we didnt march but 10 or 12 miles, we suffered for water, it has been very dry here this fall & the streams are dried up but we did get some cistern water. We helped ourselves to apples occasionaly which didnt come bad, we laid down & slept soundly without tent or covering. we never put up tents - only when it rained. The second day we were drumed up at 4 oclock, got ready to start at daybreak. the thing went about the same to day as yesterday only we didnt have to carry our knapsacks, each company teamster took the companies knapsacks the rest of the march, and an other thing the weather was cooler. all the trouble was the boys feet got sore. About now we began to get in to niggerism. we could see some kind of a niggers head stick out of every window I went in to one house where I saw 6 or 8 of the most ragged little half breeds I have seen it was a deplorable sight.—The third we got up at 3 oclock & started after partaking of a cup of coffee & one cracker. all the water we could get to make coffee of was what we had in our canteens. At 10 oclock we found a pool of quite good water after marching about 10 miles we camped here for the day, hadnt been here long before the hens, geese and turkeys began to come in together with some sheep and hogs. by this time we began to get somewhat hungry. I went to a house & bought a hoecake made out of rye flour, I gave her 10 cents & left in the afternoon & Rufus Marrel & a fellow by the name of strong went out to prospect while we was out a sheep took after me (at any rate I imagined so) & you know I was not a going to run, consequently we had some good mutton for supper & breakfast. I returned Sam Northrup his revolver with 5 charges in it. I tell you the secesh around here have had to suffer. At night we had an order not to forage any more, & then we had to stop it. The forth day we got up at before three drank our regular coffee drawed 3 crackers for 4 meals & started had a first rate day to march in the road was rough but the day was cool we got here about noon & encamped tired & hungry, but have got a beautiful place, there is about 7 or 8 thousand infantry & batteries with a suitable accompanent of Cavalry how long we shall stay here I dont know I guess our regiment will go some where to night or to morrow (the rest of this letter is missing)

Kentucky was in a difficult position during the war. The Confederates had put a star for the state in their flag, but when it came to vote for secession, Kentucky elected to stay in the Union even though it was a slave state. The war was said to be a battle of brother against brother, and never was this more true than in Kentucky. Initially Kentucky had declared itself neutral, and Lincoln had said the Union would not invade it, but when the Confederates invaded first, all promises were off. The Confederates had thought that when they entered Kentucky, the populace would rise to join them, and some surely did, but the great mass uprising that the Confederates had expected never materialized.

Since Kentucky was officially in the Union camp, foraging was frowned on by the Union Army; it was the equivalent of stealing from one's own people. However, it was all right to take cattle from a "Secesh that was droving for the Rebel army." As soon as the army entered true Confederate Territory, foraging was the rule and became a real necessity if the men were to eat.

Edgar's remark about the "ragged little half-breeds" was more than a comment about the slaves. The Richmonds and Van Nesses were conservative Protestants and considered sex outside of marriage sinful. Implicit in his statement was a condemnation of the slave owner responsible for this "deplorable sight."

Some names were very popular during this time, Emma and Sarah being two of them. Sometimes it is difficult to determine who is the lady mentioned in the letter. Emma in the following letter was Will Shurtleff's younger sister.

WILL TO MARY:

[Upside down at the top of the page] My respects to your Gibralter visitors and kindest regards to all old friends. Never presume again to apologise for writing on a large sheet of paper. It's just the sort we want.

In camp near Cynthiana Oct 18th [1862]

Dear Mary

Your letter long expected came at last. Our chaplain joined the regiment last night bringing with him the mail due to us for the last two weeks. You can scarcely imagine the impatience the boys manifested while waiting for its distribution afer it came in camp. "The mail's in" was echoed from one end of camp to the other and the mutterings and grumblings at our postmaster's tardiness were loudly and freely expressed. We are now encamped in a splendid grove of elm, maple, and black walnut, carpeted with a greensward of the famed Kentucky blue grass. The country from Covington up to Falmouth is the most miserable eyes ever beheld or if you think that is putting the case too strong I'll except the Portage sand ridges and the laurel hills of Pennsylvania; but here we are just entering the blue grass region and the country is beginning to look almost as well as Wisconsin. Cynthiana is a village about the size of Portage. There is something about the style and fashion of the buildings that I can't exactly describe but one is continually reminded by the odd-looking architecture that he is far away from the thrift and enterprise of the North. Some buildings it is true are handsome and well proportioned but in general there is displayed but little of the taste that might be expected in an old settled country like this.

You seem to wonder whether I like soldiering or not. Well to tell the truth I never have and probably never will like the hardships incidental to a soldiers life but as yet we have seen little or nothing of the sort. The weather has been beautiful with scarcely rain enough to lay the dust since we have been in the state. We had a slight frost night before last and that was the first I had noticed, so you see the trouble our friends borrowed about us was causeless. Another thing, we are in the field it is true but unless something unforseen occurs our active service will consist in hurried marches rather than in fighting. I am not sure but I do wrong in confessing as much for fear of the letter being intercepted but I am sure we are not yet well enough disciplined to risk an engagement if we can avoid it; and as far as that goes I don't think there is a possibility of anything more than a guerrilla skirmish at present. A few days ago I gave some of you a new address but the first will answer just as well until we move further south. I expected to have heard from Mattie before this time. Why hasn't she written. Our tent is full and has been ever since I commenced writing and there is so much else going on that I can scarcely write.

1/2 past eight. It is now after taps but the Cap has special permission to keep a light burning to night and I am profiting by it. I commenced early in the evening but our own tent got so full of visitors I was obliged to quit. Anything like privacy is impossible here except with commissioned officers. Chaplain Weinich gave us a sermon this afternoon that had at least one good point and that was its brevity. I have forgotten the text as usual but it was some thing warlike. Emma has heard him in Baraboo and she will probably recollect that I didn't fancy him much although I presume he is a good man enough. Contrebands are getting more plentiful down this way so much so that our little sergeant came in this morning glowing with excitement and bringing information to the effect that he knew of a little darkey we could coax to run away with us. We all agreed that it would be handy to have the fellow wash and cook for us but as we took no further steps in the matter I'm afraid he thought we slighted his proposition. I have but very slight opportunities for observation but so far as I can see the slaves here are well used. The union people I have talked with are not Abolitionists. They are as devoted to the union as any in the North for ought I know but they don't wish to have slavery meddled with. I have not heard any of them express an opinion concerning the Emancipation Proclamation. I presume they are indifferent about it as it affects only those states in rebellion after the first of January. I see by letters from home that you are considerably exercised about it up there. It may work some injustice if slavery is abolished by whole states unless the rights of loyal masters are recognized, but I apprehend this class in the far south is so small that it will make little difference either way. Well I didn't intend to talk politics to you when I commenced to write but you may be assured that I have just as much contempt as ever for Pump Carpenter, Jack Turner and all others of that persuasion. I'll try to write a more connected letter next time and remain your friend,

Will

Although Will was easily the most thoughtful and least prejudiced of the letter writers, he had a definite bias toward what he saw as the "thrift and enterprise of the North." The Yankee mindset was strongly against a man living off the labor of another man, especially when the other man was a slave. This does not mean that Will thought that the Negro was the equal of the white man, but he did seem to recognize the injustice of slavery.

He used the term "contraband" in speaking of the slaves as they were considered property that could be confiscated.

Who Pump Carpenter and Jack Turner were is unknown.

WILL TO MARY:

Nicholasville, Ky.
November 2nd 1862

Dear Mary

I have been rather negligent lately in the matter of writing letters partly because we were marching and partly because my portfolio was missing letter paper but now that I have secured such a superior article I am again your most obedient.

We have been jogging slowly southward through the "Garden of Kentucky" since leaving Falmouth. Paris is a pretty little town and the Parisiennes are what Cummings would call amiable — that is the Union portion for we have secessionists all through here. By the way I hav'n't heard from Cummings and if you should hear from him please give me his address.

You mention the death of Emma Brier's cousin. Mattie also speaks of the death of Frank Brier who she presumes I knew. There seems to be some slight insinuations implied in both that I could easily answer—in fact I have wanted to tell you before but I hardly felt justified in telling the whole truth. I am not sure now that you were not jesting about gossip that you didn't believe. If you will ask me plain questions so that I may be sure what you are talking about I will be glad to answer you. It would be rather ungallant to say the least for an old bachelor to contradict all the love stories gossips may set afloat unless he has some good reason. So much for flirting. Now I'll tell where we are and what we are doing. For the first we are in camp in a grove as usual, this time near Nicholasville. It is called Camp Price in our military reports. Camp Dick Robinson is seven miles from here. As to what we are doing I am writing to Mary. Baker is writing Chris. Stacker is writing. Corporal Yule is in here arguing theological questions so earnestly that one can't hear himself think. Some of the boys are round the camp fire but the most are in the tents trying to keep warm and amusing themselves as best they can. The weather generally except when we had our snow storm at Paris has been quite comfortable. I was on picket one cold night but we had a breakfast of hot rolls and coffee and that consoled us very materially. Our picket-station was at the railroad bridge and in the morning a doctor came down and invited part of the boys to breakfast and the rest of us went to a house near by where we had three or four *lubly cullud* ladies to wait on the table.

Nov. 4th

While at Lexington we were within a mile or two of the 22nd Wis. and when we started on the march their brass band came out and played some excellent music in compliment to their brothers of the 23rd. It seemed almost like parting with old friends. Since then we begin to feel proud enough to start a brass band too. Yesterday afternoon our major and quartermaster went to Cincinnati and one of their errands was to get a set of cornets to commence with. Today is election and if I can get the result in the regiment I'll enclose it.

WTS

The "Cummings" that Will mentioned was Brainerd Cummings, who had been a teacher in West Point during the school year preceding May of 1859 and had boarded in the Van Ness home. He corresponded with both Will and Mary after he left West Point.[5]

Will seems little testy on the subject of Emma Brier. Perhaps he had forgotten a letter he had written to Mary some time before he went into the army. The following letter does not have the year in the date but was probably written before the start of the war. It is included not only because of the reference to Emma Brier but also because it gives a flavor of life before the war and a deeper insight into Will before he had the responsibilities of a Sergeant.

Will to Mary:

Baraboo, April 5th [1860?]

Dear Friend Mary

I received your kind letter last Sunday and am very much obliged to you for that same, but please don't think me a negligent correspondent for not answering it sooner - I was intending to go over home to-day and I thought a little friendly chatting would be a good deal pleasanter than letter writing; but here am I still in Baraboo, for our April clouds have been weeping rainy tears all day long and now I suppose I must postpone my visit another week at least.

Our famous maple-sugar party came off a week ago last Saturday. Allow me to introduce our little company: first—Miss Emma Brier, the lady who graciously condescended to accompany W.T.S- rather a pretty girl, pleasant and sociable, first rate singer, schoolma'am, education ordinary, and that's all I know about her. Emma selected her as the one I should take and I was quite willing to be pleased with the selection.

Miss Addie Pillsbury, very lady-like, because she has been brought up so, well educated reads Latin, French, and German plays the piano and is ready to raise old Sancho when out of sight of the old folks.

Miss Sarah Martin, called pretty by some, education ordinary although she is reading Cicero and is nearly through Bourdon's Algebra writes pretty well and is editress of the Hesperus.

And Miss Nettie Lewis handsome but sad looking, modest and rather reserved but still very pleasant company after getting acquainted. So much for the ladies. Mr. Starks who invited us, ranges in height somewhere between six and seven feet is bashful and awkward, rather thick headed but a good fellow nevertheless.

Mr. Lewis came from Vermont last fall, has a good education now but is going through college, is pretty wild and has plenty of money.

Charlie Ferrington is a good-looking chap of eighteen or nineteen, a farmer's boy and full of fun.

Starks had led us to expect a rough backwoods entertainment saying that it was away out in the woods etc, etc, so you can imagine our surprise on entering one of the most stylish establishments in the county—carpeted parlors furnished with mahagany chairs, sofas, and tables, gilt framed mirrors and oil paintings—a grand piano, well furnished library and well I guess the list is long enough.

But do you suppose we dined with the farm hands? No indeed! our lordly selves were waited on at the table by servants under the direction of Mrs. Starks in a manner corresponding to the dignity of such august visitors. I must confess, however, that I should have felt quite as much at home and enjoyed myself full as well in a log cabin. On the way home Miss Brier complained of being cold so I drove on ahead without waiting for the rest of the company, and now listen to the cruel conundrum that came out in the Hesperus the next week: Why is S. a hard customer on livery horses? Because he drives with a frozen brier.—I have unanimously voted that Hesperus to be a wicked institution.

Give my respects, compliments, best wishes kind regards and all that sort of thing to Mattie and write soon and often to

Your Friend
W.T. Shurtleff

WILL TO MATTIE:

Camp Price, Nicholasville
Ky. Nov. 9th /62

Friend Mattie

This is pleasant Sunday afternoon, the church bells are chiming pleasantly in the village half a mile or so from camp, and here the captains are just calling their companies to "fall in" for the purpose of listening to the Chaplain, but for this time at least I prefer to shut myself in my tent and have a little chat (by letter) with old friends. I thank you for your letter but really I think I might have had more than one by this time. I wish you success in your studies and if this reaches you before the close of the term give my compliments to your friends there not forgetting Uncle Andrew. I hope you will finish that railroad in time for me to ride home — It would be rather nice to step out of the cars and find ourselves in the great and flourishing city of Lodi. How did you get the impression that I was homesick. I certainly have not been and don't know what I could have written to cause you to think so. I would like to see you all, but camp life has not yet lost its novelty and attraction despite hurried marches and hard crackers. Perhaps a smart little skirmish might spoil the fun. I'm sure I don't know. We are having some disagreable rumors in camp lately — first of an armistice then of foreign intervention, now of the hurried assembling of Congress. What does it all mean? Have they any foundation in fact or are they merely flying stories? I hope our northern politicians are not trying to force the government to accept terms from traitors. My own political opinions have not changed in the least that I know of since entering the army. It will be soon enough to show leniency to rebels when we have crushed out their forces in the field. That we are able to do it I do not doubt. Neither do I doubt that it will cost a great sacrifice but when we in the army are ready I do hope our friends in the North will not waver or hesitate. I don't know that I have much to write about ourselves. We have drills, reviews etc. pretty much as usual. I am afraid we are going into winter quarters here, but don't know yet. The boys generally are well. Charles Passage is getting better although still in hospital. Bancroft is still in Covington. We heard from him yesterday. Sergt.Stacker is writing and he bothers me to spell about every other word for him. A moment ago his pen spattered and I overheard him whisper "Damn de pen dat stick de paper." You can see he didn't go to meeting either. Kind regards to all from

Will

The Confederates were devoutly hoping that the English would enter the war on the Confederate side, the theory being that the English cotton mills could not do without Southern cotton to keep them running so it was in the English interest to be for the South. However, while the English did want the cotton, they were also against slavery. When Lincoln put forth the Emancipation Proclamation, he effectively made it impossible for the English to enter the war on the Southern side as to do so would have made the English seem to be supporting slavery.[6]

When Will talked about an armistice or possible foreign intervention, he was referring to a proposal by the French emperor,

Napoleon III, to England and Russia that the three countries propose an armistice to the warring parties. The English and Russians turned the emperor down, feeling that the time was not right.

THOMAS TO MATTIE:

Camp Price Nicholasville
Kentucky Nov 10th 62

Friend Mattie

Not having recieved a letter from you for to long I thought I would run the risk of incurring your displeasure by writing you once more. Have you written and your letter miscarried or have I offended you. If I have offended you I hope you will write me and let me know as you know suspense is worse than the knowledge of the wrong. I was some what sick last Night and went out on a drill this morning and that made me feel still worse so the Captain Excused me this afternoon and I thought I would improve the time by writing. I think by Resting this afternoon I shall be all sound for drill again to Morrow morning. We have had some long tedious marches since I wrote you last. I stood them first rate. We passed through some very pleasant pretty Towns Paris Especially is quite a pretty place and it is also a good Union place we were cheered there the best of any place on our march. The young Ladies waved the Stars and Stripes over us almost all the way through town and I tell you such things cheer us up a good deal when we are tired and hungry.

Lexington Is rather an old looking place but is Noted as the Home of one of our old Statesmen Henry Clay. There is a splendid Monument erected to his Memory. I can not tell you the exact size but from the distance I saw it from I should judge it was forty feet square at the base and a Hundred feet high. His Statue is cut on the top in the Attitude he would occupy in making a speech. We are now in the First Division first Brigade and the first Regt in the Brigade Under Major General A J Smith and Brigadier General Burlbridge.

We have had what they call two Grand Reviews. Nothing very grand for us High privates but I suppose it looks very well to the Spectators.

There has been Considerable talk about our staying here for Winter quarters til this morning but now they seem some what undecided about it. If they want us to do any fighting I wish they would march us right along and let us fight now if there is no fighting to be done I hope they will let us stay were we are for we are very well situated here.

Now Mattie I want you to write and tell me all about the trouble if any there is and about how you enjoy yourself at School.

Give my best respects to Mary and all enquiring Friends and believe me to remain truly

Your Friend
Thomas

Please Direct

Co H 23 Reg
Wis Vol
Via Cincinnati Ohio
To Follow the Reg

Thomas said that Lexington was a "rather old looking town," and it probably did look old as it was settled in 1779, making it 84 years old when the 23rd Wisconsin went through it.

On November 11 the regiment left Nicholasville and marched to Louisville, a little over 80 miles. They arrived on November 15 and on November 18 embarked on the steamboat *Sir William Wallace* for Memphis.

Will to Mary:

Louisville Ky.
Nov. 16th /62

Dear Mary

Yours of the 5th was received after we had commenced our march from Camp Price and since then I have not had a moments time for writing until now.

We started Tuesday morning and reached Louisville about noon yesterday (Saturday morning) coming by way of Versailles, Frankfort and Shelbyvile making the distance about eighty-two miles. Our camp is west of the city near the canal and the surroundings remind one quite forcibly of the flats below Portage. We marched through town but I was too tired to pay much attention to its looks, however its general appearance did not impress me very favorably. If I can get a chance I am going up town to look around but I don't know yet how long we shall stay — in fact don't know when or where we are going. Nashville, Vicksburg and Texas are among the different places mentioned in camp. Versailles is one prettiest little villages I have seen. Frankfort lies in a narrow valley with steep rocky bluffs on either side. I can give no good description of it, however as we have very little chance for sight-seeing on a march and particularly in marching through cities the file closers have about as much as they can attend to in keeping the gawkies from gaping and staring around and blundering out of their places in the ranks. There will be some in any company who have no pride in their own appearance or that of the regiment. I see by looking towards sunsetting that we are North instead of West of the city.

You will perhaps think strange after what I have written about winter quarters at Camp Price that we should move back here but I can give no explanation. The order for moving came about 11 o'clock Monday night and we were on the road at daybreak Tuesday morning. Here we expect pay and full supplies, then we are to march some where — perhaps you up there can tell our destination better than we. Now abruptly good night

WTS

EDGAR RICHMOND TO ADELINE VAN NESS:

In camp near Louisville Ky Nov 16 [62]

Dear Sister

I take this favorable opportunity to answer your kind letter which I received when we were at Nicholasville.

I wrote to Dave a day or two before we started that I thought we should stay there through the winter as we had been ordered to fix up for cold weather but all at once we were ordered to march to this place a distance of 86 miles thus proving that we cant calculate with any degree of certainty upon anything of an earthly nature. We arrived here last night after a march of 5 days over a McAdamized road or pike. these roads are hard as a rock & in fact they are made of stone pounded up to the size of your fist, & become like a solid rock after a while consequently we naturaly had the legs ache the first day or two but I feel this morning more like traveling that I have any time yet. How long we shall stay there is no telling but probably not long. We expect to go down the river somewhere, some think to Nashville some to Texas & others to Vicksburg we cant tell nor do we care much providing we get enough to eat. We have marched about 200 miles in this state & I cant see what it has amounted to. Get your map & follow us around commencing at Covington & bringing it up at Louisville by the way of Independence Falmouth Cynthiana Paris Lexington Nicholasville Frankfort Shelbyville & from there here. They tell us there has a Brigade a day left here for several days for the south. the Union

Morgan is expected here every day with his army to go farther south. I guess by the time we all get there they will begin to think there is some men up north.

I cant write much more at present but will write a gain after we get to our distination. Tell Ma I am all right & just about as good as ever & I will be around in a short time & we will have a gay old time in that new house. Tell Ike he must do the fiddling this winter for the dances. Tell little Walter that Uncle Ed wants to see him very much, and ask him whats trumps.

I must close & go to dinner the infallible coffee & cracker but there no need of eating crackers to day for I will bet there is 500 women & children in this camp selling bread & cake etc. I will put in some Locusts seed. these big ones are sweet locusts. these small ones are black locusts.

From your Brother Ed

PS Direct to Louisville Ky. Be shure to put in the regiment & company & put at bottom.

P.M. Forward to regiment

Thomas to Mattie:

Nov 17th 62

Friend Mattie

Your Kind letter of Oct the 25 came to hand this morning. I had just made up my mind that I was never going to recieve another letter from you but as the old saying runs better late than never. We have had some long tiresome marches since I wrote you last. We left Nicholasville a week ago to Morrow morning arrived here about one o clock Saturday the most of us pretty well tired out. I will tell you the names of the Principal Towns we passed through that you may see the Rout we took. Our first Nights rest was at Versailles after that we passed through Frankfort Shelbyville and quite a number of small towns hardly worthy of Note. I was very much disappointed on entering Frankfort. I thought as it was the Capitol of the State of Course it must be a very nice place. But instead of that it is a small dirty little town Built down in a hole and hemmed in by high Bluffs with no chance whatever to grow. In fact there isnt room for it to stretch itself when it wakes up in the morning. Shelbyville is quite a pretty place. Louisville is quite a large place but rather dirty and smoky looking. How long we shall stay here No one seems to know or where we shall go or anything about it.

There has been two Funerals out of our Brigade this afternoon one poor fellow out of the 96th Ohio and one out of our own Reg Co A. I have just been out to see the Funeral Procession. Ed was one of the Musicians it looked rather Sad and Solemn. This was the first Death in our Regt. You told me in your letter to be a good boy. I dont want you to tell me to do any more impossibilities. As you may well know that is one.

I recieved a letter from Sarah this Morning One from My Mother and one from a Brother that is in the Army near Washington. I had not recieved a letter so long that it cheered me up considerable. I will write you again soon. I have to close now on account of tie for I have to answer the others before leaving here if possible. Remember me to all enquiring Friends. Best Regards to Mary and Accept My best wishes for yourself and believe me to remain

Truly your Friend
Thomas Townsend
Direct Co H 23 Reg Wis Vol
Louisville
Kentucky
PM Forward to the Reg

On June 8, 1861, the Sanitary Commission, an independent citizens' group, was formed to help maintain healthy conditions for the troops including caring for the wounded, improving their diet and living conditions, coordinating supplies sent to the troops, and other things that would improve the lot of the soldiers. There was much to be done. Many of the soldiers had little or no knowledge of sanitation. Diseases directly traceable to contaminated food and water, such as typhoid, were rampant. Sometimes, as in the 23rd's march from Cincinnati to Falmouth, the men suffered so for water that they drank whatever was at hand, clean or not. Of course it could be contaminated even if it looked clean. Will's worries about the health of his men and their possible sicknesses were well founded.

WILL TO MARY:

Louisville, Kentucky
Nov. 18th 1862

Dear Mary

I Wrote to you but a day or two since but as it is a rainy day I shall have leisure to trouble you again. I went to the city and am willing now to admit that it looks much better than I at first supposed. We didn't march through the handsomest part of the city in coming to camp. One thing I observed in town and that was the great number of hospitals and sick and wounded soldiers. Many of these soldiers are destitute of money and of course must depend entirely on hospital stores and from the little I have seen of hospitals I judge convalescents can get very little that is palatable. A well man can endure almost any sort of diet and cookery but the best is none too good for the sick whether at home or in camp. Now a word concerning your aid society. We expect to move down the river very soon and probably without pay. Many of our own company are without money. I have lent more that I ought to have done to accommodate some until payday. The weather is bad and at this season of the year is likely to continue so and what I fear is that if we stay on the river many of the sick will need things they have no means of obtaining until sent from home. I have no doubt the friends of Co H would be glad to send these things if they knew how to do it safely. A few days since Co F received a box marked "Sanitary Goods. Care of Capt Schlick, 23d. Reg.Wis.Vol.Inft. Nicholasville or elsewhere". I think a similar direction would bring a box to Company H. by way of Cairo. You know better that I what sick people need. It must be recollected that in camp their bed is straw spread on the ground. I have sometimes seen it recommended to send goods directly to the Sanitary Commission but in such a case you can tell nothing about where they will go. If sent to a company in care of the Captain or some proper person you have the satisfaction of knowing who is aided. I have written to you under the supposition that your father would be willing to mention the matter to citizens of West Point and Lodi and see what can be done. Little items sent to particular individuals might be marked and sent in the same box. Don't misunderstand me now from what I have already written. There has been no suffering in our company that I know of and perhaps would not be if nothing were sent. I would merely make the suggestion and let our friends act as they think best.

The Colonel has this minute announced in camp that we go on board transports at 3 o'clock P.M. This cuts short a long letter I intended to write as I shall be obliged to go to work immediately. I may perhaps have time to write to Clara and Emma after getting on board.

Remember me to old friends.

WTS

3

Down to Memphis

In the summer of '62, in a series of battles, Grant opened the Mississippi River as far as Vicksburg, Mississippi. Control of the Mississippi was important not only as a pathway for supplies for the Union forces but also to keep the Confederate forces from being supplied. Since some of the railroads in the South had been destroyed by Confederate forces in retreat, the river was the only quick way to transport troops, although quick is a relative term, as Edgar's letter makes clear.

Edgar to Adeline:

To Adeline Van Ness
Camp near Memphis Nov 28th [62]

Dear Sister

I thought I would write a few lines to let you know where I am & how I get along. As you have already heard no doubt we started from Louisville the 19th of Nov on board the Sir Wm Wallace bound for this place as it appears. We landed yesterday about 11 oclock A.M. after being closely confined for 8 days. We had rather bad luck while on the Ohio river on account of low waters & the many sand bars. We ran on to one & was most all day getting off. When we got on to the Mississippi we came right along without trouble. We are all well with the exception of bad colds which most of us catched at Louisville. We are getting over our colds some now & will feel better after dinner.

Gen Shermans army left here yesterday for Holly Springs. He has 40,000 men. He has gone there to give Bragg battle. A large fleet of gun boats left here 2 or 3 days ago for Vicksburg and we expect to march again after the Brigades get together. I think by the appearance of things there is to be some thing done this winter. I must close now & put this in Ansons Letter because I have no more postage stamps. I have received no answers to the letters I wrote to you & Ike, and Dave & George & Sarah yet. When you write again put in a drawing of tea. A good many letters come to the army with tea in & that is some thing I havent tasted since I was in Camp Randall.

From Ed

P.S. Direct to Memphis via Cairo P.M. Forward to Reg.

When the men of Company H boarded the transport at Louisville, they did so in a pouring rain which soaked them to the skin. They had no chance to change clothes and stayed in their wet things until they arrived in Memphis.[7] The bad colds which Ed Richmond and Gib Reynolds "catched" at Louisville turned into bronchitis, and both men were left in the hospital in Memphis.

In a time of antibiotics it is difficult to realize the inroads disease made, not only on the soldiers but on the general population. Even in the 1930s pneumonia was the leading cause of death in the United States. Many times the difference between life or death was the quality of nursing care, something the army woefully lacked. Over twice as many soldiers died of disease in the Civil War as were killed or died of their wounds.

The standard treatments for bronchitis and pneumonia at that time were bleedings, doses of opium and quinine, and mustard plasters, which were poultices made of crushed mustard seed and applied to the chest. Quinine, which was a specific treatment for malaria, was not only used for respiratory infections but for stomach aches, diarrhea, and practically everything else.

THOMAS TO MATTIE:

The following was a four page letter, approx 8x10 sheet folded in the middle to make four pages. The bottom half of the first page and top half of pages 3&4 are missing, torn off neatly, the letter being held together by a strip about 1 in. in the center.

[in pencil at the top of the page]

Sweet are the ties of friendship true
But soon on earth they're over
Yet sweeter far when found anew
Before the throne of heaven

Memphis Tenn Dec 16th 62

Dear Friend

I have just Recd your kind Letter of Nov 19th and sit down to answer immediatly. I think this is rather old News dont you A letter of Nov 19th Recieved Dec 16th. We Recd a lot of old mail to day that has been lying back ever since Oct. We are now at Memphis as you are well aware of probably. But we are expecting to move down the . . .

Made a good fireplace. I tell you we are fixed quite cozy here and another thing we get our mail pretty Regular here that is quite an object with us Soldiers. I Recd a Letter from Milton Yesterday with six Dollars in. I tell you that will come Nice for we have been out of Money for a long time now.

I will freely forgive you for writing with a pencil. I shall be perfectly well satisfied of I can only get letters no matter what . . .

We have had a first rate time since we have been here. Have lived well and not done much. Our QM has had a good Brick Oven built and we have had good Soft Bread almost all the time besides having potatoes and Fried Beef every other Day Very high Living for Soldiers. Last Friday We had another of those Grand Reviews Our Camp is about Two miles from Town And last Friday we started for Town in a Rain Marched all . . . way, if not I say Fight to the Last.

Our Colonel thinks that We shall have Peace in A Month from now and I think his Opinion is worth a good deal either in time of War or Peace. I See my sheet is almost full So I will bring this scrawl to a close. Give My Best Respects to Russel and Family. Tell him I shall write him soon but I do not think I have Waited quite as long yet before answering his as he did before he answered mine. Give my Best Respects to Your Parents. Kind Wishes to Mary and Believe Me to Remain Truly Your

Friend Thomas Townsend
Direct to Co H 23 Regt Wis Vol
Memphis Tenn PM Forward to the Reg

Please write soon

4

The Yazoo, River of Death

After two weeks of good food and not much work, the 23rd was made part of the 1st Brigade, 1st Division of Sherman's Yazoo Expedition. The mouth of the Yazoo River was just above Vicksburg and ran in an easterly direction for a few miles before it turned and ran to the north-east. Grant's plan was to head up the Yazoo for a few miles and then turn south from the Yazoo and approach the east side of Vicksburg from the north. It was impossible to attack Vicksburg from the river as it was situated on a high bluff. On the other sides it was pretty much surrounded by swamps which the Union troops had to get through to attack the city. As can be seen from the following letters, the plan did not succeed.

Will to Mary (?)

Up the Yazoo
Saturday evening Dec.27 [62]

(no salutation)

I have seated myself on the deck just outside the state-rooms with an empty cracker box for a writing desk—well I've got so far and the order is "fall in."

Jan 4th 1863 You see as usual it takes some time to finish a letter after I've commenced it. We had just made a successful raid to Dallas station on the railroad from Vicksburg to Monroe in Louisiana & I was intending to tell you about it but now it is rather an old story. On Christmas morning our brigade started out from Buckhorn Landing arriving at Dallas about seven in the evening.

Our object was to destroy rail-road bridges and cotton. At the depot where we camped we enjoyed one nights rest on uncounted pounds of downy cotton. The whole ground occupied by our regiment was covered by its fleecy whiteness contrasting broadly with the sable countenances of sundry darkies who were reveling in their first day's freedom & trying to make themselves useful whether bidden or not. After finishing our work we started back at noon reaching the boat late at night. Distance 30 miles. Next day we dropped down to the mouth of the Yazoo & sailed up that river twelve miles. This brings me to where I commence this letter. Late in the evening I got things fixed for writing thinking to take advantage of the quiet while the rest were sleeping but instead of that we were hurried off through the mud & darkness to take a position before the rebel works. About seven miles out we kindled small fires & laid on our arms until awakened about four o'clock by heavy firing on our left. At 9 A.M. we moved forward & took a position near the bank of the bayou but as it happened were not brought into action. The firing was kept up nearly all day. No accident happened in the 23rd although sometimes a shell would come close enough to make one feel nervous. I understand Steele's Division suffered severely & Morgan's considerably but I can get no particulars Nothing was accomplished. This was Sunday. On New Years day preparations were made for retreat & at night we came back to the boats. we are now 30 or 40 miles up the river - have met Gen. McClernand what the next move is I can't say. Grant has fallen back. This gave the rebels reinforcements & deprived us of expected support. I am rather unwell. Dr. Irwin says I have the measles. I have not heard from you in a long, long time. Why is it. A large mail came in today but I only had a letter from George. Pardon this pencil scrawl for really I am too sickish to write. When I get over the measles I'll try to do better.

Remember me to all. As ever your friend

WTS

Will was absolutely right when he said that Steele's Division suffered severely. Five hundred men were killed, wounded or captured when the enemy struck it. The total Union loses were heavy, with over 1,200 killed or wounded and over 500 captured or missing. The Confederate losses totaled 207.

While measles is usually considered a childhood disease, it was rampant among the country boys during the Civil War as many of them lived in isolated areas and had not been exposed as children. One account says that 1,700 Confederate soldiers were ill with measles just before the first battle of Bull Run.

After the defeat on the Yazoo, Sherman had the idea of taking Fort Hindman, forty miles up the Arkansas River at an outpost called Arkansas Post. His superior, General McClernand, easily agreed as both were anxious for a victory to help erase the memory of the defeat they had just suffered. On January 8 they set out.

WILLIAM TO MATTIE:

Arkansas Post
Jan 13th 63

Friend Mattie

I haven't the conveniences for letter writing but try & pencil a few lines as there is a mail going out this morning. I have been unwell a few days but I'm now almost well again. Our boys have had a battle here & taken a fort called Arkansas Post. I was too sick to recollect much about what they were doing until Sunday. They left the boats sometime on Saturday (10th) & drove the rebels from one or two positions but on Sunday the fighting commenced in earnest. The gunboats & field artillery shelled the works until the middle of the afternoon when their guns were mostly silenced. Our infantry had been gradually closing up at favorable opportunities until within rifle shot and then they kept under cover & picked off the gunners. Toward night they prepared to charge bayonet & carry the fort by storm when the rebels ran up the white flag & surrendered. I believe we have between five & six thousand prisoners with a considerable amount of stores ammunition etc. In our company Lt. Holdridge had his ancle slightly bruised and Tom Yule his knee badly shattered. His leg has been amputated. Poor Tom. I disliked him at first but after getting used to his peculiarities I was beginning to think a good deal of him. His soldiering is over & I hope he will soon get home again. The loss in our regiment was I think 4 killed and 34 wounded. They are hurrying up the mail & I must close. Please write often. Remember me kindly to all.

WTS

In the following letter to Mattie, Thomas gives his version of the trip up the Yazoo and the taking of Arkansas Post. The Black Swamp was in the area south of the Yazoo. Like all of the swamps in the South, it was full of malaria-carrying mosquitos, and malaria took its toll on the soldiers. This letter is the first indication that Thomas has been infected, although he simply says he has been unwell. The intermittent attacks of chills and fever characteristic of malaria become evident in his later letters.

THOMAS TO MATTIE:

On the Mississippi on Board
the Steamer John H Dickey Jan 18th 63

Friend Mattie

I do not know but you have forgotten there is such a body as myself living for I have not heard from you for such a long time. We have had considerable work to do since I wrote you last and may have considerable more to do before I get a chance to write you again for I believe it is the intention of Our Generals to move on to Vicksburg again as soon as possible. We were down there once but had to retreat for want of reinforcements. I hope we shall be more successful if we go there again. It came very near proving the ruin of the 23 Regt when we were there before for we lay five days in a nasty low swamp without our tents and while there it came a drenching Rain wetting us very nicley in consquence of which our Regt is nearly half sick at the present time. I have been quite unwell myself ever since we first went into the swamp until within a few days ago.

After leaving the Swamp we came back up the Arkansas and took a Secesh Fort Capturing everything General and all the Generals name is Churchill. You will probaly have a great deal better account of it through the Newspapers that I can give you of it. Our Brigade was not Landed until Saturday Afternoon and by the time we had got our position it was dark and the Firing had almost ceased for the Night. Sunday Morning We lay on our Arms ready to go into action at a Moments Notice. About Noon Our Regt was ordered to the Front and up we jumped and started. We had not been on foot more that ten minutes before A Cannon Ball came whizzing along just grazing the Captains leg and then Striking Corporal Yules Leg Shattering it so bad that it was taken of immediately. The Corporal was the next Man to me on my right hand and I thought it was pretty Careless shooting to throw the balls so close as that. We were firing for about an hour and after we once commenced I felt just as cool as though I was at work on the Farm. After firing about an hour our Regt was relieved by another one and we were ordered to the rear to rest ourselves and make ready for a Bayonet charge right into the Fort. But just as we had got nicely rested and were just got into line again ready for the Charge the white Flag was seen waving over the Fort and the Fort and all there was in it was ours. I believe there was about a thousand Prisoners. It was a good Haul. They were qurious looking Soldiers to us every one has his own Uniform to suit himself. You could hardly tell the Privates from the Officers. There were one Hundred of our Regt Came very near being taking Prisoner a day or two after the Fight we were detailed to go up the River about Fifteen miles above the Fleet with a little old Tow boat to get a Load of Secesh Corn we got up were the Corn was about Four oclock and found that it was impossible to get the Corn and report back to the fleet in the morning as we were ordered to So we set fire to the Corn and were almost ready to leave when a band of Guerillas popped out of the Woods and gave us a regular hail storm of Bullets which storm we returned as fast as possible. Two of our men were wounded and three of theirs Killed. Five of our Men were out on the bank when the Rebs fired in to us they were out looking for Chickens our Boat was cut loose and we started down the River and left them and suppose of course that would be the last of them but escaped and have got back safe and sound. I do not know as I told you how we spent our Holidays. Christmas Morning we were called on to go away out into Louisiana on a Bridge burning Expedition. We left the Boat about nine oclock and started for the Rail Road Bridge we marched and marched and marched and marched till about nine oclock in the Evening when we arrived at the long looked for Bridge and railroad and there we stopped for the Night after making ourselves a cup of Coffee apiece we went to work making ourselves beds by tearing the Cotton Bales to pieces of which there was over a thousand and making ourselves as comfortable as possible. The next morning we were up bright and early, and went to work tearing up the Rail Road and burning the Bridge and Depot. About Noon we left for the Boat again destroying all the Secesh Cotton we could find all the way back Arrived back at the Boat about Midnight as tired a lot of Men as any one ever saw After Marching between fifty and sixty Miles and doing a good deal of work inside of forty hours. So ended our Christmas

The next morning we were started for Vicksburg and New Years day we spent in the Black Swamp with nothing to amuse us or attract our attention excepting now and then a Rebel shell would coming singing through the tree tops and burst at a little distance from us. That was New Years so much for so much. Edward Streater has been quite sick but is getting a little better now. I am in hopes he will out and around again in a few days. Edgar Richmond and Gilbert were both left in the Hospital at Memphis sick. I said Nothing about it before as it was against Gilberts wishes to have any one write that he was sick. We have not heard from them since we left Memphis so how they get along is more than we are able to say. I hope they may be better. Will you please tell Russel that Edward has been quite anxious to hear from him in regard to the Affairs With Uncle Jesse. How does Jimmy and Emma get along now. Have they forgotten the time they were in Madison or do you Remind them of it occasionally just remind them of it for me will you.

I am going to put a little Cotton in this that I picked in a cotton Field in Louisiana on Christmas day also a little moss that hangs on almost all the trees in the swamps down here and gives them a very pretty appearance now that the Leaves are all of. It has been very Cold here for the past few days there was about four inches of snow fell three or four days ago and it has been quite cold here ever since.

I have just about run out for something to say so will bring this to a close by sending my best wishes to all enquiring Friends. Give my best Respects to your Parents also to Russel and Family. My best wishes to Mary and yourself and believe me to Remain Yours Truly

Thomas

Please write soon sooner soonest

Direct Memphis Tenn
PM Forward to the Regt

There were three common kinds of cannonballs used in the Civil War. One exploded either in the air or on impact. Another was an iron ball that was blown through the air by the force of the gun powder but did not explode, and the third was a canister which had the effect of shrapnel.[8] It was the second type which struck Corporal Yule. A Richmond family story was that one of the men of the 23rd lost his leg when he tried to stop the ball with his foot as it rolled on the ground, not realizing the force that was still in it. If this was Corporal Yule, Thomas either did not see the corporal receive his wound, or in deference to Corporal Yule, did not mention such an embarrassing occurrence.

Sometime in the previous two months Edgar Richmond and Gib Reynolds had been transferred from the hospital in Memphis to the general hospital in Mound City, Illinois, just north of Cairo, Grant's base. The Emancipation Proclamation was signed January 1, and many soldiers were saying that they enlisted to save the Union, not to free the slaves. Edgar seems to blame the desertions on the Proclamation, and many men must have used that as either a reason or an excuse, for desertions in the Union Army ran about 1,200 a week or 5,000 a month and continued to do so through 1864. Considering that a man could be shot for desertion if he were caught, the number deserting was enormous. In 1863 the problem was so bad that Lincoln declared amnesty for those who returned to their units and served out their enlistments.

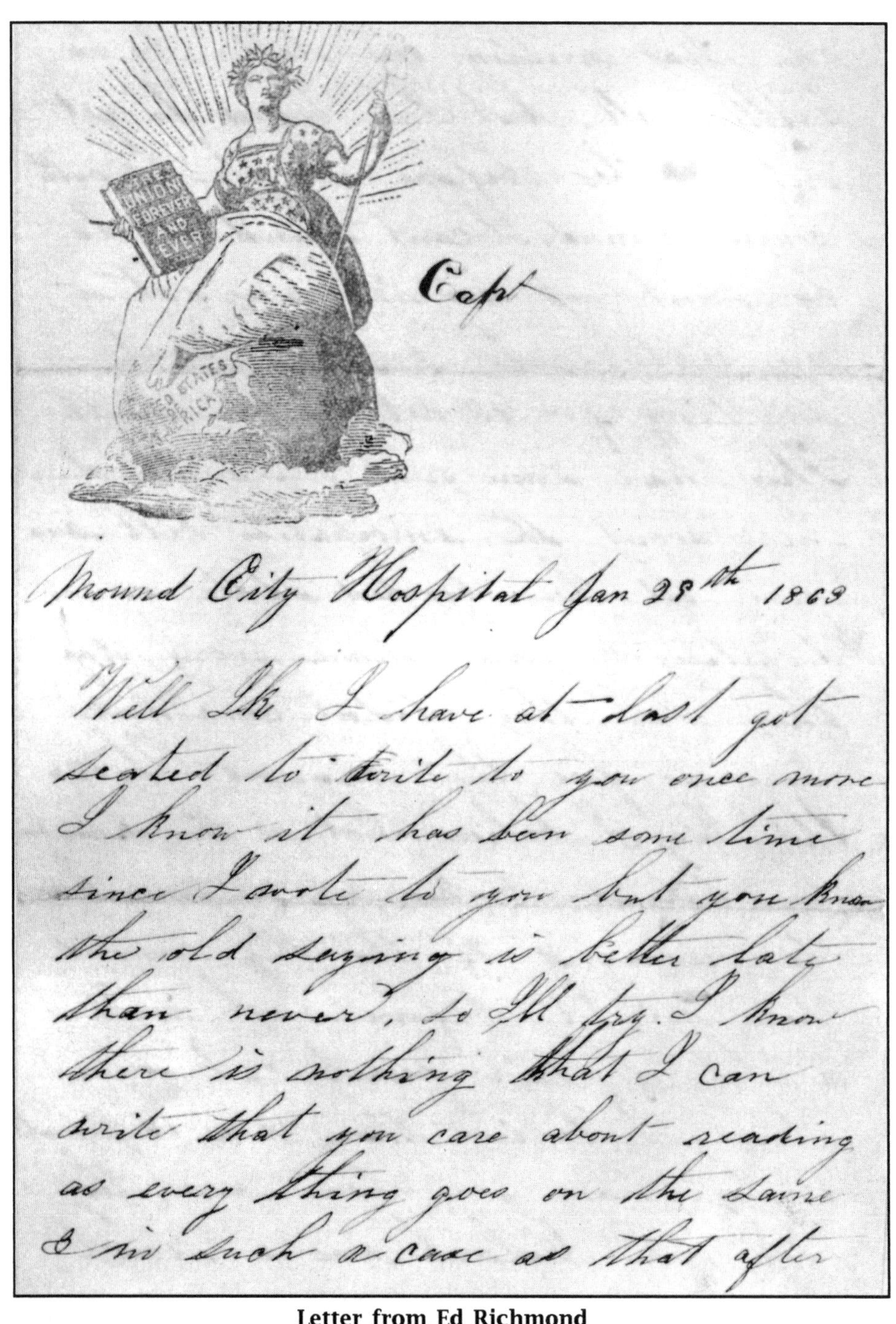

Capt

Mound City Hospital Jan 28th 1863

Well Ik I have at last got seated to write to you once more I know it has been some time since I wrote to you but you know the old saying is better late than never, so I'll try. I know there is nothing that I can write that you care about reading as every thing goes on the same & in such a case as that after

Letter from Ed Richmond
January 28, 1863

Private collection of Susan T. Puck

The slaves that were freed as a result of the Union Army's movements through the South followed the army in droves. Illiterate, underfed, and in rags, they posed a real problem for the Northern troops. Hearing from the Southern papers that the freed slaves were eating food meant for the soldiers and remembering the times they had been on half rations or less must have destroyed what little morale the hospitalized soldiers had left.

EDGAR TO ISAAC VAN NESS:

Mound City Hospital Jan 28th 1863

Well Ike I have at last got seated to write to you once more. I know it has been some time since I wrote to you but you know the old saying is better late than never, so I'll try. I know there is nothing that I can write that you care about reading as everything goes on the same & in such a case as that after one has written one letter he has written all, but Im bound to get out of this before an other month comes around. I cant stand it to be shut up in this way. It is my nature to be busy about somthing for 12 dollars a month They have some great old times down here about the emancipation bill men from all these borded states are deserting & going home every day they say they didn't come down here to free the niggers. The 128 Ill Reg I believe that is the number has entirely broken up & gone home The remains of the Reg landed here night before last with a lot of their quartermaster stores. I believe there was 16 privates & they have gone home now. they say the Colonel was a secesh they said he enlisted for both sides at the same time so as to make out his regiment. he is arrested now. The niggers are thick at Memphis. I take it according to some of these southern papers they state that thousands of half starved naked wretches are flocking in to that place. they are of all ages from 8 years to 100 but not many among them that are able to work. they are taken care of: the niggers are following up our armies wherever they are, consuming the food that our soldiers ought to have & defering on helping our armies back on their marches

Ike I think I am about as good as a nig & if I can get out of it I am a thinking it will be some time before they get me to enlist to free niggers.

A part of Gen Grants army has moved down the river to act in conjunction with Mc Clernand in the subjugation of Vicksburg. I hope they wont have another Bulls Run of it

Now Ike I want to talk to you a little about getting transfered. I would like to have you & Reynolds see the Governer & have him call Gib & I to Madison. Some of the soldiers tell me that where any body is transfered to their own state, they have to pay their own way, but I dont believe it.

If I could get near home as that Madison wouldnt hold me long. Gib wants to get home bad as me, & if we cant do it one way we will an other, if you have time I wish you would see about it before you write again. I will make it all right with you when I draw my money.

From Ed

Edgar's information about the 128th Illinois Regiment was essentially correct. After five months of service, the unit was so decimated by desertion that it was disbanded by order of General Grant, with the few remaining men absorbed into another unit. The officers, deemed "utterly incompetent," were mustered out.[9]

While Ed's desire to get home was mostly motivated by boredom and homesickness, it made good medical sense. Good nursing care and a nutritious diet were far more available with one's family than in an Army hospital, and at home one would not be shut up with dozens of other soldiers with many different maladies, communicable and otherwise.

Uncle Jesse was Jesse Van Ness, brother to Peter and uncle to Isaac. Both Jesse and Peter were active in the affairs of the community.

EDGAR TO ADELINE:

Mound City Hospital Jan 29 1863

Dear Sister

I received your letter about 10 minutes ago & as I am writing to Ike thought I would not write very extensively to you for it is all the same. I received the money safe and sound. There was more than I expected. I thought if I got one dollar I should be satisfied, but I guess I shant loose it. If I should happen to get transfered to the Hospital in Madison it will come good on the way. I asked the Doc this morning if they ever done such thing as to transfer sick men to their own state he said yes sometime. I think the shurest way to do is if I could someone that is acquainted with the Governor & have him call us to our own state. I think Un Jesse would have influence. If I could get as near home as that it would be a good deal with me as it is with Harve. If I had my descriptive roll I am almost shure I could get a discharge but it is lost & there is no certainty of getting another if I should write again. If I did get it would not be under a month & I dont want to stay here another month.

I am about the same in health, but I have got so sick of laying & sitting around with nothing to do & have to think that this is all caused for a nigger that I cant stand it. I must close by thanking you all for the money & all your kindness. Tell Walter I would like to see him bad as he would me.

Ed

Whether the governor had anything to do with it or not is unknown, but Ed Richmond was discharged on the tenth of February and sent home. Gib Reynolds preceded him by a few days.

THOMAS TO MATTIE:

On Board the Steamboat
Fanny Bullit
Feb. 15th 1863

Friend Mattie

Your kind letter of the 3inst was recd and read with much pleasure on the 13th. The part of Our Regt. that is fit for duty is once more on there way up the River. In Fact all Our Brigade is going up. The Report is that the Rebels are in Force some where above here on The River bank and we are going up there to see what can be done. I think it is quite Likely there is fun for us ahead. I remembered you to W. Shurtleff and he was wondering why you had not written So I told him the reasons that You gave me. He said I was to Remember Him to you and to tell you that He thought it was quite a Joke on the Directions.

You were wondering why you had not Heard from Sarah. I think I can tell you the Reason. She has been very ill with Dyphtheria. The last time she wrote me she had to be bolstered up on the Lounge with Pillows and since then I heard through one of Edward Streaters Letters that She was considerable worse. I hope she may be so that she can write to you again ere this. You wished me to write you about how I felt at being shot at in the Battle. I do not know how to Describe my Feelings when on our way to the battle ground. But one thing I know and that is that I thought of more there in the same length of Time than I ever did before. Thomas Yule was the next man to me on the Right and it was but very few minutes after he fell that I felt as cool and composed as it were possible for any one to feel under the Circumstances. I can tell you it is no very pleasant thing to be marching along through the bushes as we were and to hear those Shells come whizzing Screaming and tearing through them like some angry Spirit Seeking Revenge. After we got into Action I thought no more of danger. It was load and fire and make my Shots Count if Possible. As soon as we got within musket range the Bullets flew thick and fast but as a general thing they were almost harmless for they were over our heads but still they sing no pretty tune. Our Camp is now in full view of the Rebel Strong hold Vicksburg. How long they are going to keep us in camp there without doing any thing I do not know but we have been there now nearly a month and nothing done yet excepting that we have the pleasure of digging on the Canal or some poor levee once in a while. The fact is the large Army of the Missisippi has Dwindled away till it is almost gone. This is an awful Country to bring Northern men into and I hope we may soon get out of it. My health has been very good so far Compared with most of the Company. I have not been Excused from duty on account of Sickness yet Since I Enlisted.

Not if I Remember right And there are but few in our Company that can say that. Edward Streater was very Sick at the time of the Battle and for a long time after. He had the Typhoid Fever. He is almost well but is not doing duty yet. There is a great deal of Sickness amongst the troops but I think a great deal of it proceeds from Low Spiritedness or Homesickness just as you have a mind to call it.

One thing We are all out of Money and that makes it far worse than it would be if we had a little Money by us to get some little dainties From the sutlers when we get out of sorts.

We hear that Gilbert has got his Discharge. Lucky Boy. I am glad that he did not leave Memphis to come down the River to join the Regt for if he had he would have found that to be the time his troubles commenced. The first time you see him give him my best respects and tell him not to forget his Old Comrades for I shall expect a letter from him soon after I hear that He is at Home.

You tell me I must not get Disheartened. I try not to but sometimes when these Shoulder Straps put on so many airs and try to Show there Authority so much it makes me feel as though I should like to hasten that day when we shall once more stand on equal footing with them and tell them what we think of them as we will do should we ever live to return to Lodi. I will now draw this to a close till I see what this Expedition will amount to so Good Bye for to day.

Five miles below Naplon [Napoleon]

Friend Mattie

I will now try and finish up this uninteresting letter. I told you on the other sheet that I thought there was Fun for us ahead. I found out by experience that there was but it was rather to hot and muddy for this Child. Our Boats landed the next Morning after I wrote you and we were ordered to be all ready for a march with three days Rations in our Haversacks. About Eleven Oclock we started and marched all day through a drenching rain and such mud as I never saw before in my life and about five oclock at Night we had marched Eight Miles and were almost tired to death. That Night we took Possession of two of the Largest Plantations I have seen yet and there we made up for our Hard days work by Confiscating all the Chickens Turkeys Geese pigs and Cattle that we wanted to eat. Besides that we had lots of Honey Molasses Corn dodgers and Sweet Potatoes. I tell you we had a good Supper and Breakfast. Besides Chicken and other things I drew I made out to confiscate a first rate India Rubber Overcoat just the very thing for that kind of Weather. The Next Morning about Nine oclock we started back for the Boats and such a Tramp as that I never want to take again.

We arrived back Safe at the Boats about four oclock and all the Rebels I saw or heard of were three that our Cavalry took. So much for a Sixteen mile tramp through the mud and the rain. Yesterday morning we again started up the River and stopped here about dark last Night. This Morning there has been a large Foraging party sent out on Horses and Mules. I hope they will bring in something good to eat for our Rations are running Short.

Feb 27th [or 29th]

As I have had no chance to post this I have had to keep it with me and now we are back to Camp again. Our Foraging party that went out met with quite a large band of Guerillas and sent back to the Boats for Reinforcements So the 23 was sent out at almost a double quick the Cavalry Reported that they were only about Four Miles from the Boats but we found they were fully eight miles out. We started about Noon without taking any thing to eat or without our Blankets or Overcoats we had quite a little skirmish with them and drove them and I tell you they skedaddled about as fast as there Horses could carry them and the 23rd after them but they were to fleet for us and just at dark we gave up the chase and tried to find us some thing to eat but we were in a very poor place as far as eating or sleeping was concerned. We found a very little coarse corn Meal and saw some Hogs running around some little log Shantys out of that we made our Supper and breakfast and next day we started back for the boat and all we Captured was one small cannon that they had to leave in there Hurry to get away from us. Since then we have been chasing them away from the River up or down wherever we could find them. Yesterday we got back to camp but I dont care how soon they take us back for it is fun to chase them fellows and Forage all through the Country for a living. I will now bring this to a close for I am afraid your patience will be exhausted before you have read half of this scribble. Give my best respects to all enquiring Friends and believe me to remain as ever your Friend

Thomas Townsend

PS I have just recd another letter from Sarah she has been very dangerously ill so much so that one time they thought that every breath she breathed would be her last but she is getting better and I hope you may hear from her soon. She had Typhoid fever with Diptheria. She must have been very sick but I hope she will soon be well again. Direct the same as before

Good Bye

Thomas was complaining about commissioned officers when he used the term "Shoulder Straps." An officer's rank was indicated by an insignia on his shoulder strap which ran from front to back near the seam where the sleeve joined the jacket. Thomas was probably talking about the same officer that Will complained about later.

At about this time Mary Van Ness had been hired as a governess at the Reynolds' household. Gilbert (Gib) Reynolds had just arrived home, which is the reason Will makes a remark about romance in the following letter.

Correctly used, the term "sutler" referred to a civilian who had been appointed by a regimental commander to sell things to the regiment that the men weren't able to obtain from the regular stores. Each regiment was allowed one official sutler. However, the correspondents of the 23rd Wisconsin seem to use the term to refer to anyone who followed the army with items to sell.

WILL TO MARY:

Young's Point, Feb.19th [63]

Dear Mary

Yours of the 27th duly received. I am very glad to hear of your own good health and thank you kindly for your good wishes concerning mine even though they are included under "etc. etc." "Oh, I love to hear the patter of the rain upon the roof," but when it comes to pattering for successive days and nights on a miserable leaky tent the sensation isn't quite so agreeable and this for the past few days has been our experience. To-day it is sunshiny again and looks and feels quite spring-like. Our brigade went up the river last Saturday on some sort of an expedition I have not learned exactly what and I not being wither sick or well have ignobly staid in camp. It may be a satisfaction to Clara and Emma to know that I am not always with the regiment although to tell the truth but a small part of the regiment is in the field- this time company H numbered twenty-six all told. Holdridge is captain now, more is the pity. He received his commission just after the capture of Arkansas Post.

A governess indeed! I wonder what chapter of romance will happen now. Hope you may have the measles again if, as you seem to intimate, it would give you an assurance of beauty. And Mattie a teacher in the Lodi Seminary under the special supervision of Andrew G! S'pose that's the reason she hasn't written but I can't help it now. Dear a me!

We have no news - doing nothing but trying to exist though the dullest kind of camp life - eating our rations when we are well enough to relish them, if not paying unconscionable prices to sutlers for little delicacies - these I believe are almost the only features to be recollected of this part of our sojourn in Dixie. What the next few weeks may bring about I can't say but I must confess that the troops generally have lost confidence in our leaders and even interest in the cause for which they enlisted. While we regret all this we can scarcely blame them, for official mismanagement and this detestable climate is enough to discourage almost any one.

Feb. 23rd I don't recollect why I stopped writing but I guess it was for fear of getting the blues after going on in such a lugubrious strain. I will try to think less of such matters unless it is fervently to wish that negroes and emancipation proclamations may soon disappear from American politics forever. Perhaps I ought to say here that we have very few abolitionists amongst us. We would fight for the honor of the old flag and the preservation of the Union but not for the negro. If emancipation will aid in suppressing the rebellion we will say God speed, but we do not profess to be endowed with much of that stay-at-home philanthropy that would do so much and sacrifice so much merely for the freedom of the poor negro.

My latest dates from home are from Emma of Feb. 10th & 11th. I was pleased to hear of Gilbert's safe arrival and that Ed was expected soon. If they should forget to write to me I hope you will jog their memories.

Our brigade is not yet back. Grant is said to be opening a canal 75 or 80 miles above here into some lakes and bayous leading into the Red river and thus make the attempt to get below Vicksburg with his boats in that direction. The canal here is progressing favorably but the rebels have heavy batteries opposite the mouth and below.

I expect to come back there some time in June to eat strawberries and cream and besides I shall take occasion to scold some if you don't write oftener. By the way, in looking over your letter the somewhat formal "Mr.-" "Dear Sir" etc. suggests that I have been too familiar in addressing you; if that is the case please let me know.

As ever your friend
WTS

5

DISASTER AT VICKSBURG

After the Yazoo Expedition, the 23rd Wisconsin was transferred to the 1st Brigade, 10th Division, 13th Army Corps, Army of the Tennessee, and in early March was moved from the Yazoo camp down to Milliken's Bend in Louisiana, north of Vicksburg, Mississippi. Grant had put the men to work digging canals, one at Young's Point and one at Lake Providence in Louisiana, just south of the Arkansas border. Grant's idea in digging the canals was to try to get below Vicksburg with his gunboats by some alternate route, as running the Mississippi would put them under bombardment from the cannons on the bluffs at Vicksburg. Also Grant believed in keeping the army busy when they weren't fighting, and digging canals certainly did that.

WILL TO MATTIE:

Milliken's Bend, March 2- th [1863]

Dear Friend Mattie

Yours of Feb 23d was duly received but I fear judging by your example that I am answering it too soon. The situation and prospect of the 23rd has greatly improved since your writing. You must no longer think of us as being utterly prostrated by sickness. A good camp, good water, and the substantial kindness of friends at home is fast bringing back our health and spirits. We are at least out of sight if not beyond the influence of the Yazoo or "river of death." Our experience through January and February seems like a frightful dream. Thank Heaven that our prospects are now brightening.

Last Saturday we received our boxes from Lodi. For particulars I refer you to the Lodi Herald as Lieut. Baker has I believe made out a full report. I believe he intends to keep the people of Lodi and vicinity posted concerning our movements through the medium of the paper.

I am sorry you had heard nothing of my Selina but I will hope that by this time you have had better fortune. Perhaps I oughtn't to confess it (to you) but any information concerning that lady would give me infinite pleasure.

Alonzo Avery has been stationed at Lake Providence and he writes to his brother in the 23d that the canal at that place is a failure, the rebels having cut the levees to flood the country and thus prevent clearing out the bayous. The water burst through the embankments at Young's Point before that canal was finished and according to the boys Gen. Grant said it "might go to hell now for all he cared." So it goes. When I find out that we have really done anything down here I shall be glad to let you know. Kind regards from your friend *Will*

Please write oftener

Will's letter to Mary requesting supplies for sick and wounded men was dated November 19, 1862, and the material arrived the middle of March. Since the regiment had moved from Louisville to the region of Vicksburg and had been fighting much of the time, the delay must have been frustrating to the Lodi people who were worried about their loved ones. Their joy at finally reaching the troops was only equaled by the joy of the men at receiving tangible proof of the care and concern of the people back home.

WILL TO MARY:

Milliken's Bend, La. March 27 [63]

Dear Mary

Yours of the 13th came duly to hand and found us greatly improved in spirits and circumstances. In fact we begin to think we are somebody again. We are beginning to have visitors too. First the paymaster came to gladden our hearts, after months of weary waiting, with a few precious "greenbacks." Then came Messrs. Wolcott and Treadway with the Sanitary Stores and our famous and never-to-be-forgotten Lodi boxes. Yesterday the Eleventh landed near us and "made a break" as the boys say, for the twenty-third, officers and guards to the contrary notwithstanding. Horace

Polly came over and staid all night with us. His health is good - he says it never was better than since he has been in the army. Finally, last evening Dr. Lewis Blachley of Lodi came trudging into camp carpet-bag in hand in company with several other volunteer physicians from Wisconsin. I was not personally acquainted with Blachley but it is quite a relief to see even a stranger from the north. It seems now as though the people of Wisconsin were fully aroused concerning our wants and in no wise backward in endeavoring to supply them. There is a heavy force concentrating here and everything seems to indicate a speedy forward movement of our hitherto inactive Army of the Mississippi. To be sure we have little opportunity for gaining information concerning contemplated movements but we hear that a large number of light draught steamers are preparing or perhaps by this time have gone through the Yazoo Pass carrying what I suppose they call the left wing of the grand army down the Yazoo thus giving an opportunity for attacking the defenses of Vicksburg in the rear. You will no doubt recollect that last winter our gunboats were unable to pass the batteries at Haine's Bluff. This compelled us to attack in front with the odds altogether against us and the consequence was defeat.

You inquire about Holdridge but I don't know that I have much to say except that I have a dislike for the man. I will give one or two reasons. While at Young's Point I was quite unwell and excused from duty by the surgeon. Our regiment was ordered off on a foraging expedition and although the captain was perfectly well aware of my illness he gave me peremptory orders to fall in. We were gone several days but of course I was unable to do anything and remained on the boat the whole time. He merely wished to exercise a little brief authority. Several similar instances have occurred to my knowledge. I submitted rather than to make a scene before the company although both the Lieutenants advised me to complain to the colonel. Lately he has been "good as pie." I am inclined to thing he has received a lecture from some source on such matters. Baker's health is improving so that he now reports for duty. I presume Dr. Irwin will have arrived at Lodi before this reaches you.

I had heard some time since of the revival in West Point and although I may be prejudiced I confess the news did not give me much pleasure. My experience in prayer meetings has often been similar to what you relate and I believe in such cases I came away worse instead of better. There is a quiet, unassuming every-day Christianity that I can respect and love, but I have no confidence in the spasmodic and transient results of so-called revivals. You ask whether I have written to Tish. I have not yet but I will try to if

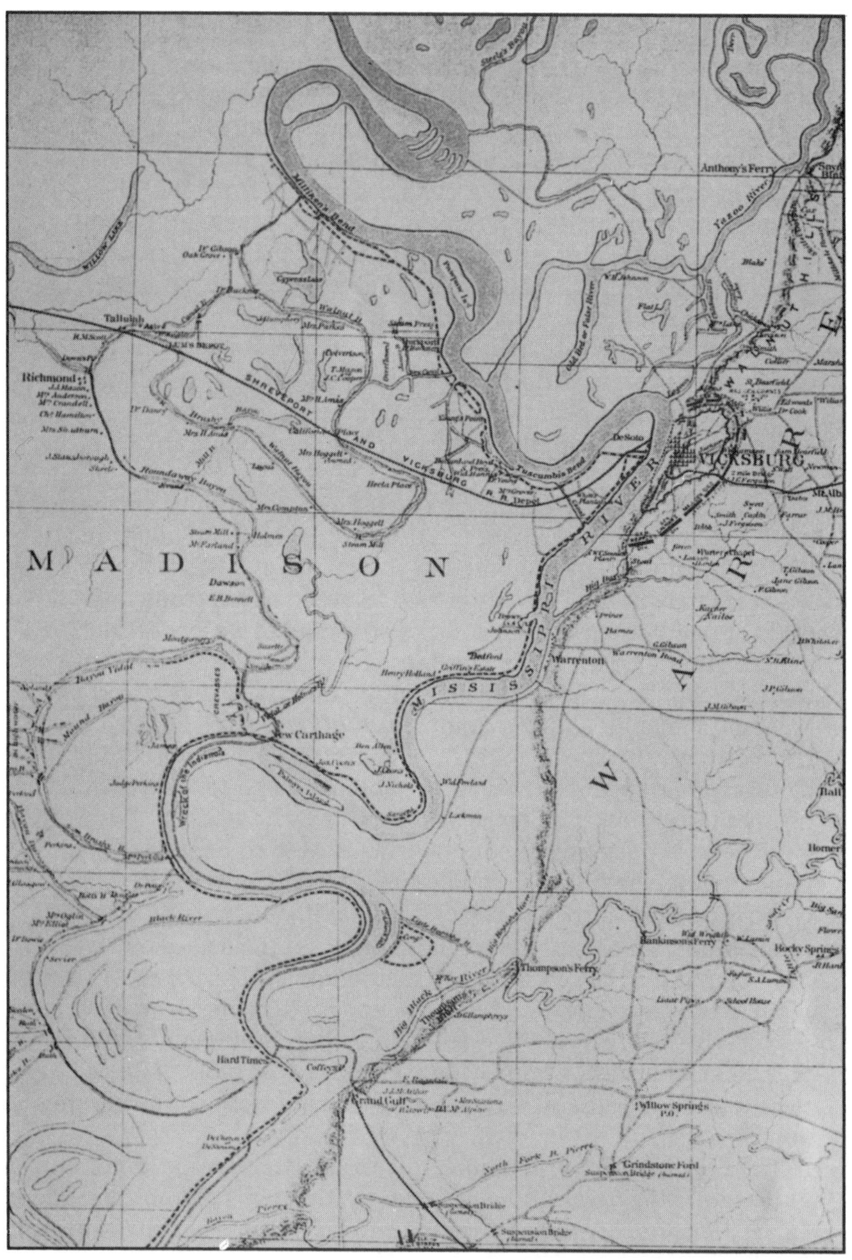

Vicksburg area section of the map showing the country from Milliken's Bend to below Vicksburg, Mississippi, from *The Atlas to Accompany the Official Records of the Union and Confederate Armies.*

Courtesy The Bancroft Library

I can get time. I did not suppose she would care particularly to hear from me so I had thought little or nothing about it.

I am glad we think so nearly alike about the unnecessary formalities of letter writing. Hence forward we can each write as we please without fear of giving offense. A kind good bye and regards to all from Will

---

The Yazoo Pass expedition that Will mentioned was a failure, and the boats had to withdraw after taking a pounding from the Confederates. All of his other tactics having failed, Grant decided to get his troops to the east side of Vicksburg by marching them down the west side of the Mississippi, ferrying them across below Vicksburg, and marching them back up the east bank where they could approach Vicksburg from the east, the only possible direction from which to storm the town. About the time of the withdrawal of the Yazoo Pass expedition, the 23rd Wisconsin left Milliken's Bend and headed south through the Louisiana mud.

THOMAS TO MATTIE:

April 10th 1863 Grassy Camp Louisiana

Dear Friend

Onward to Vicksburg will probaly be our motto now as we have left our camp at Millikens bend. Last Tuesday morning we had orders to pack our Knapsacks and put three days rations in our Haversacks and be ready to march and about three oclock in the afternoon we started Marched out about four miles to an old Cotton Gin and stopped here and made our selves Comfortable for the Night. Next morning found us on the road again bright and early and by Noon we reached a very pleasant little village called Richmond.

There we were allowed to rest and had a bite to eat. We called it dinner. I dont know what you would call it But we were soon on foot again and were kept marching pretty much all the time from then till Night And we found then that we had marched between fifteen and twenty miles since morning with our Knapsacks and through some of the worst Mud Louisiana can afford. From here I believe we go to Carthage some fifteen miles below Vicksburg and there cross the River to get in the rear of the Butternuts as I hear there is one Division crossing there now. They had a little Skirmish some where near here yesterday before we arrived and report says that one of our Indiana Colonels were killed. But the Rebs were routed and drove two or three miles and two of there men were taken Prisoners. I do not know whether my correspondents are still in the land of the living or not as I can not hear from them but if you are and should get this will you please let me know as I feel anxious to hear from some one as I have not recd a letter now for over three weeks. You must excuse me for not writing a long letter this time as I have quite a number to write to and we are now were we are liable to be called any moment. Our Pickets were fired on here Yesterday.

Give my Best Respects to Russel and Family. Tell him my Health still continues good. With Kind Respects to your Parents Brothers and Sister I will close Hoping you are well write soon and Believe me to Remain

Truly Your Friend
Thomas Townsend

Direct as usual

Grant finally decided to run the blockade of the Mississippi with his gunboats, as without the boats there was no way to ferry his troops across the wide Mississippi below Vicksburg. On the night of April 16, under the leadership of Admiral David Porter, the first run was made with seven gunboats, three transports loaded with stores, and a steam ram. The boats took a total of 68 hits, but only one transport was sunk and no one was killed. Other runs followed in the ensuing days.

THOMAS TO MATTIE:

Louisiana April 24th 1863

Dear Friend

I think it must have done a good deal of good for me to scold so in my last letter for yours of the 8th was recd in a very few days after my scolding letter left here. I am scribbling this with a lead pencil as you will plainly see but the reason is that I am on Picket to day and my ink is in Camp. The Weather is extremely warm here although I am very comfortable at the present time as I have a kind of a rail pen built up and covered over with a blanket and some nice green Boughs. You wished to know what we do odd spells. We do some very lazy Lounging around and for my own part I do considerable sleeping these warm days and then bother the other Boys after they get to bed at Night. Quite a disgraceful occurrence took place in our usually quiet Regt on the Night of the 22nd. As there had been quite a number of Promotions amongst the Commish of late they made up there minds to have a little spree and as a matter of Course they used the Liquor rather freely. Some of the more sensible ones knew when they had drank enough and retired but they were not allowed to rest for the others went and dragged them out of there tents and forced them to take another glass. Amongst them that had gone to there tents was the Head Surgeon and they tried a long time to get him out but he would not go upon which they began to tear his tent down on him and he told them to stop and leave him alone but no they would not until he drew his Revolver from under his Pillow and fired into them Severely if not Mortally wounding Captain Greene of Co D. The Doctor has made tracks for parts unknown so much for an Officers Spree.

Our Troops are busy crossing the River below Vicksburg. Report says that two Divisions are already across. Running the Blockade is getting to be a thing of frequent Occurrence. Three Gunboats and five Transports ran the Blockade the Night before last six transports started but one found a Watery Grave verdict[:] Cause Rebel Cannon balls. We are still in Camp were we were when I wrote You last About twenty miles from Millikens Bend and ten from Carthage. I do not know when we shall move from here. I have not heard anything about it the last day or two but I suppose we are liable to go at any minute. I saw Horace Polly just before we left the Bend. He was well and looking tough and hearty.

Alligators are quite plenty here the Boys have Captured several they are very pretty things. I wish I could send you one in a letter.

We have but very little drill now that the weather has got so warm and the 23rd seems to think the less the better. Do you ever hear from Sarah. I have not heard from her for over three weeks. I am afraid if we get across the Mississippi our Mail Facilities will be very Slim and they are bad enough now.

Perkins Plantation Apr 30th 1863

Just as I had got Comfortably fixed and got to writing we recieved Marching Orders and were called in of Picket to start down de Riber and we are now below Vicksburg. Our Forces are all going down to Grand Gulf at the Mouth of Black River were they expect to have quite a Battle. Our Regt went down the day before Yesterday. I had been quite unwell for a few days so was left here in charge of Company Property. But I hope I shall be well enough to join them in a few days for it seems lonely to be away from the Co. We had reports from the Gulf last Night our Gun Boats had silenced nearly all There Batteries and they expected to attack them with the Infantry today. If we succeed in taking this point we can burn the Rail Road Bridge across Black River and cut of there supplies. There is very heavy firing now up the River either at Vicksburg or Warrenten it is almost a continual roar of Heavy Guns.

The Plantation we are on here is a splendid place the most Beautiful place I have seen anywhere on the River. It is owned by Judge Perkins a member of the Rebel Congress. He laid His Mansion in ashes at the time our Forces Captured New Orleans. William Shurtleff recd a letter from Gilbert a day or two ago and in it he spoke about Em and some young Gentleman having quite an interesting time. I wish when you write you would give us the Particulars if they are not a secret. As you know well enough I am very anxious to know all about it. Poor Em. I think it is too bad dont you. W.S. is getting quite strong again he looks better now than he has for four months past in fact he looks quite rugged once more.

May 4th 63

Our troops have taken Grand Gulf and are on there way to Jackson they Captured some fifteen Hundred Prisoners over four hundred of them were marched by here this morning they look hard. I feel some better than when the Regt left but I am rather weak. We are expecting Orders to move down to Grand Gulf as some are already going. I have not heard any particulars in regard to the Regt but am almost crazy to know if they were engaged in the Fighting or not. We expect the mail will leave this morning so I will close this hoping that I shall be able to inform you in my next that Vicksburg is in our possession. Remember me to all enquiring Friends and believe me to Remain truly

Your Friend Thomas

Captain Greene, the random victim of the surgeon's wrath (and pistol) survived the shooting and was a major at the end of the war. What happened to the surgeon is unknown.

After the battle of Port Gibson on May 1st, the 23rd Wisconsin went on to participate in the Battle of Champion's Hill on May 16 and the Big Black River on May 17. May 18 found them facing the ridge at Vicksburg. The first assault on May 19 failed almost as soon as it started. However, Grant still thought the ridge could be taken. After trying to batter the Confederate defenses with shells from gunboats on the river and cannon from the other side, Grant ordered the army to attack at ten in the morning on May 22. The result was a disaster—3,199 fallen, including 649 killed or missing.

THOMAS TO MATTIE:

Near Vicksburg May 27

Friend Mattie

I will send you a few words just to let you know that I am still spared to render a little assistance in the Reduction of Vicksburg. I left Perkins Plantation to Join the Regt soon after writing you last and overtook the Regt soon after the fight at Grand Gulf. Since then we have done a good deal of Marching and fighting and we are now lying close to Vicksburg and the Big Guns are booming away day and Night. Our Forces made a Charge on the Forts and got up close to them but could not get in So were obliged to fall back to were they started from it was a Murderous thing and many a hundred good and Brave men Yielded up there lives on that day. Mattie I have bad News to tell you but I may as well be plain. Poor William Shurtleff is badly Wounded. I am almost afraid Mortally. Phirm Stahl is Dead and many others of our Co Wounded. I was not with them in the Charge as I was not able. I had been quite unwell and was very weak in fact I am quite weak now. I have lately been Detailed to assist in the Recieving and issuing Ammunition For our Division. My Duty is lighter than it was with the Co and I hope to gain my strength. It went rather hard with me to hear of so many of our Co being wounded the Night they fell back. It was a little more than I could bear for all at once things looked dark to me and I fainted away. I hope I may never hear of so many being hurt again. I tell you it has made our Regt smaller than ever and it was very small before.

I am in hopes we shall soon be in Vicksburg for I do not think the Rebels can hold out much longer There Supplies and Communication is all cut of and we have them drawn in to a very small place for so many of them. Remember me to all inquiring Friends and Believe me to remain as ever your Friend

Thomas

[a note in pencil] The Doctor says William is gaining. We are in hopes he will get well. Good Bye

---

After the battles of May 19 and May 22, the Union Army was unable to retrieve its dead and wounded because of the murderous fire from the defenders of Vicksburg every time someone ventured onto the field. Finally on May 25 General Pemberton, the commander of Vicksburg, proposed a truce to General Grant so that the wounded and dead could be removed. Grant agreed and the casualties were retrieved. Whether Will lay wounded on the field for three days is not known. Thomas would probably not have told Mattie anyway. The news was bad enough as it was.

THOMAS TO MATTIE:

Rear of Vicksburg June 5th 63

Dear Friend

I hardly know how to commence this letter or what to say when it is commenced for I Have to write on a subject that must be alike Painfull to you as it is to my self. Poor William Shurtleff is Dead. I went to the Hospital to see him the Night before he Died but he was so low then that he hardly recognized me and could not speak at all. He must have suffered terribly for his wound was awful. The Ball entered his face near the Nose and came out Back of his Ear.

I tell you Mattie it is such Sights as are to be seen at the Hospitals that makes ones Heart sick and makes him wish that the Cruel War was ended and that we could all return to our peacefull Happy Homes.

When will this War close I often ask myself this question but can not answer it. Lieut Baker has all of Williams Private Property and I presume he will send Home all that he can the first opportunity that offers. I am afraid it will be almost a death blow to his Parents. But I hope it will be some consolation to them to know that he was faithfully performing his duty when he was called to meet his Maker.

We have not succeeded in taking Vicksburg yet. Neither do I think we ever shall by Fighting. But we can starve them out some time if it is six months hence for we have them completely surrounded both by Land and Water.

I should have written you of Williams Death before now but I have had Charge of a train for drawing Ammunition and had to see to the drawing and Issuing and it has kept me going almost Night and day. But I have had a few moments Leisure to day and have tried to improve the time by writing this

But I am afraid it is very poorly done for it is the first time I have ever been called on to write about any such thing and I Sincerely hope it will be the last.

Our Cannons are Booming almost all the time but the Rebels are so well Fortified that our Shots have but very little effect on them. The Rebs seldom ever reply to any of our guns now so that they are not doing us much damage at present. I must close as it is getting so dark I can hardly see my writing. With kind Regards to all enquiring Friends and My Best Wishes for Yourself I Remain Your Friend

Thomas Townsend

Write Soon

Will Shurtleff lived for ten days after he was wounded. Whether he would have survived with modern medical care is problematical, but under the conditions at Vicksburg it would have been miraculous. The wound may have become infected, but even if it had not, the bullet probably shattered the roof of his mouth. Since Thomas says he couldn't speak, it is possible that he couldn't swallow either and starved to death or died of thirst.

Back in West Point, Mary Van Ness carefully clipped a small newspaper notice and pasted it on the inside of the back cover of *The Songs and Ballads of Sir Walter Scott.* It read

Died
In camp, rear of Vicksburg, on the 2nd of
June, wounded the 22nd of May, WILLIAM
T. SHURTLEFF, of the 23rd Regiment, Wis,
Vol., aged 27 years and 23 days.

THOMAS TO MATTIE:

In rear of Vicksburg, June 27th 63

Dear Friend

Here we are still in the rear of the Rebel Stronghold and still at work Bombarding both by day and Night. We still keep advancing on there Works our Rifle pits are up almost close to there Forts now and I think there will be another trial of there Forts in a few days. Genl Logan has undermined one of there Forts and put in a large quantity of Powder to try to blow it up but it did not do them much damage but he is still at work and is qoing to give them another trial and I hope will meet with better Success. I am still at my old Post in the Ordnance Department and do not get much time to write so do not Blame me if I do not write a very long letter for I have half a dozen letters to answer to day for to Morrow I have to go the Yazoo River in Charge of a large train for Ammunition and I want to write a little to all to day if Possible. You have probably seen by my letters ere this that my wound was very Slight on my part although it was very severe on the Boot however it struck my boot so and missed my foot is almost a miracle to me but I am very thankful it was no worse.

Of course you will have heard of the Death of Poor William ere your recieved this. His troubles are at an end.

It was but a few days ago that we lost another young man from our Company. He was Shot dead while on Picket. His Name was John Bates. I hope this place will soon be taken for every day adds to the list of the Killed and Wounded.

I recd a letter from Sarah a few days ago. She talks some of coming down to see me during her vacation wouldnt it be pleasant to see her here. My Health is improving. I begin to look and feel as I used to once more. I hope it may continue good now. We are hearing some very Gloomy News from the Eastern Army again. When will they get to work and whip out those Eastern Butternuts. I think sometimes it will not be untill after the Rebs get in to Washington. Then I think the people of the East would turn out and drive them yes clear to the Gulf of Mexico.

How is the Weather in Wisconsin it is somewhat warm down here. Rather a warm Climate I should judge from what little experience we have had here. It is reported here that Port Hudson has been taken but we hear so much such talk that we do not know whether to believe it or not but I am in hopes it is so.

When you See Ed Richmond please give him my best regards tell him that I think he has forgotten that there is any one left in the 23rd that he ever knew.

I see Horace Polly quite frequently now as there Regt is only a short Distance from ours. He is quite well he asked to be Remembered to old Friends in West Point. Remember me to Gilbert and tell him I should like to hear from him. Give my best respects to Mary. Tell her I am going to write her a letter a yard long when we get into Vicksburg and that will be soon. Accept my best wishes for Your Self and Believe me to remain Your

Friend Thomas

Unless the soldiers received specific answers to their letters, they were never sure if the people back home received them. Thus Thomas was not completely sure Mattie had heard of William's death.

Thomas was right when he said they would not take Vicksburg by fighting, but the town was kept under siege with its food and supplies cut off and surrendered on July 4, 1863, the day after the Battle of Gettysburg. General Grant called the surrender of the city the turning point of the war. Vicksburg did not celebrate July 4 again until 1945.

THOMAS TO MATTIE:

Near Vicksburg Miss July 29th 63

Friend Mattie

I Suppose you think that I have entirely forgotten you by not writing you ere this but No Mattie I have not forgotten you.

Just as Vicksburg was taken we had Orders to get ready to go to Jackson and of Course we had to take a large train loaded with Ammunition And the work of getting it ready fell almost all on to me so that I had no time to think of such a thing as writing. At last I was ready and started and for three days and Nights I was scarcely out of the Saddle long enough to eat much more to Sleep the Result of which was that on arriving Near Jackson I found myself in a very High Fever And such a place to be sick. No care No Nothing for Nearly a week. I lay Almost Crazy and not a mouthfull of any thing could I eat at last they got ready to start back to Vicksburg and myself with quite a number of other Sick were tumbled into one of Uncle Sams Army Wagons and three days of such riding as we had there I never want to have again. But I am here and gaining strength slowly. We are Camped Near the River just below the Town but how long we shall stay here I do not know. I heard to day that Our Corp was Ordered to Natchez but do not know wether to believe it or not.

They have just commenced giving Furloughs. I have tried to get one that I might go Home and Recruit my wasted strength but I see no show at all for me at present as there are so few going at a time.

I can not learn any thing in regard to Williams Death more than his Wound was of such a Nature that he could not speak. I saw him myself the Night before he Died but he could not speak to me poor Fellow his Sufferings must have been awful. I am sorry I could not have been with him all the time he was Sick but You know we can not do as we would here. So we have to do the next best that is do as we are told.

I can not give you any reason for Sarahs not writing to you. I am sure she can not be Offended at you for She always spoke of you in the Highest terms whenever She spoke of you to me. I guess all she needs is a little scolding. There are no Flowers of any kind here where we are Camped now but I will try and get some to send you in my next. I am in hopes now that I shall be able to keep up a better correspondence with my Friends that I have done lately but If you could only know how we have been marched and Shoved around since the Taking of Vicksburg you would not wonder that I have not written more.

Vicksburg is rather a Forsaken looking place and bears a good many marks of our Cannon. I think now if our Army in the East will only take hold and do as good work as we have done here this Cruel War will soon be Brought to a close. But I put but very little Confidence in the Eastern Army. I see my sheet is almost full and it is very near dark so I will say good Night give my best Respects to all enquiring Friends and Believe me to Remain

Truly Your Friend
Thomas Townsend

Excuse bad writing for my hand is very unsteady

Thomas Gets Leave

Thomas did receive a leave in the middle of August. The cyclical nature of his illness can be seen in the following two letters. Fortunately quinine was available for its treatment; even so, over 12,000 men died of malaria during the Civil War.

Fort Wagner, mentioned in Thomas's next letter, was on Morris Island in South Carolina about a mile and a half from Fort Sumter in Charleston Harbor. General Quincy Gillmore led the attack. Among the Union troops was the 54th Massachusetts Volunteer Infantry, made up of Negro soldiers with white officers. They proved conclusively in this assault that black soldiers would fight as bravely for their country as any white soldiers, and die just as bravely, too, when the assault was repulsed by the Confederates. Brainerd Cummings was also at Fort Wagner.[10]

THOMAS TO MATTIE:

Buffalo Sept 12th 1863

Dear Friend

I have not recd your answer to my last But I feel almost sure that you have written So shall take the Liberty of writing to you again.

I am at home now but I left word with Edward Streater to Forward all letters to me So that if there is one from you any where down there I shall soon get it.

I Presume you have heard ere this that I had got a Furlough. I have been Home about three Weeks. My first thirty days would have run out next Tuesday but the Physician that has attended me

Extended my Furlough until the 14th of October as I am not well enough to go back. I have been very Sick Was quite Sick all the way Home. I had to lay over five Days at Indianapolis as I was quite unable to travel. I am Still very Poor and Weak but I am just commencing to get around.

I am going to try very hard to visit Wisconsin on my way back. If I do You can look for me there in about two weeks or a little over. Sarah has commenced teaching again so that I do not have much of her company but I undertook to Scold her for not writing you. Why says she Mattie owes me a Letter, so I had to stop Scolding.

It seems strange to me to be here as here it is so Still. Sometimes I almost feel lonesome and feel as though I wanted to be back with the Co. But then again when I think of the Hardships we have to Endure I think Home Sweet Home is the place. But If my health will permit I shall return to my Regt a willing Soldier the Middle of next month. For I can now see that our just cause is fast gaining ground.

We are very much afraid that we have lost one Brother. He was at Charleston And we have not heard from him since the first attack on Fort Wagner. He is either killed and buried by the Rebels or else a Prisoner. We are in hopes that he may be a Prisoner.

I will close this hoping that I may soon be up there then I can talk instead of writing that will be much easier and quicker. Remember me to all Enquiring Friends. Give my Best Respects to your Parents

And accept my Best Wishes
From your Friend
Thomas Townsend

Several of the letters from Thomas mention Jimmy and Em. They were James Richmond, Ed's cousin, and Emma Van Ness, a cousin of Mary and Mattie. What kinds of goings on caused all the gossip may only be imagined, but Jimmy and Em were married on January 28, 1864.

THOMAS TO MATTIE:

Buffalo Oct 5th 1863

Dear friend

I presume you have been looking for me in Wisconsin long ere this but I am Sorry to say that I shall have to give up my intended visit there As the Ordnance Officer wrote me that I had better come back by the Way of New York. They were then at New Orleans but expected to March in a day or two Either for Mobile or Galveston. By going to New York I can go to my Regt on the Government Boat without Cost and you know that is quite an Item to any one that has to work hard for a living

I am sorry to have to go back without seeing you and the rest of my friends in Wisconsin But I do not feel as though I Can Afford to pay out so much Money as it would cost me to get out there and back.

I am happy to say that my Health is improving although I am far from being Strong yet I tell you I have had a pretty Shaky time of it but I am in hopes now that I have Shook the Chills all away. If I keep as well as I am now I shall Start for New York about the Fourteenth of this Month.

I saw Sarah yesterday she is quite well she still keeps on Teaching. I have had some Photographs taken and will send you one and should like very much to have a likeness of You. Wont you send Me one (yes) Did I hear you say yes Or was it a Dream. I think you will say yes this time. I shall hope so anyway

We are having very disagreeable Weather here just now Cold and Rainy. I think it is about time for me to start for the Sunny South. I shall Freeze up here.

Wont it be to bad if Lizzie should get married before I get back If she should I hardly think I should ever get Over it what think You. If You could only hear me Sigh while I am writing about it I surely think you would pity me.

I am sorry to hear such a story about Em. I used to give her Credit for a little sound sense but I think She must have lost it now if she ever had any. And Jimmy is not much if any better, But then I suppose its all for Love what do you suppose.

Please write me soon after recieving this. With kind Regards to Mary I remain

Truly Your Friend
Thomas

PS Since writing the above I have had three more Heavy Shakes. I am almost as poor as ever. I saw Sarah yesterday. She sends her best respects and says she will write you in a day or two. I have had another Shake and have Seen the Doctor. He tells me that if I want to live I must stay here, and he wrote me a Certificate Saying I should not be fit for Duty for the next Sixty Days if as soon as that. He advises me to send for my Discharge but I think I shall wait a while longer as I am in hopes to be able to go back and try it again. Please write me soon and direct to Buffalo.

Yours in haste Thomas

Thomas was treated for his "heavy shakes" in Buffalo, then at the post hospital in Rochester, New York. He started to rejoin his regiment, but on February 1, 1864, he was admitted to General Field Hospital, 13th Army Corps, in New Orleans, Louisiana, and on February 12 to Marine General Hospital, also in New Orleans. He did finally rejoin his regiment on March 4 but was discharged April 13, 1864, on a Surgeon's Certificate of Disability.

After Thomas recovered from malaria, he got a job in the Buffalo Post Office as a clerk. The 23rd Regiment Wisconsin Volunteers continued fighting in Louisiana and Texas. In the spring of 1864 they took part in the Red River Campaign commanded by General Nathaniel Banks. Their Confederate foes were under the command of their old opponent in Kentucky, General E. Kirby Smith. On April 8 came the Battle of Sabine Crossroads in which the Union forces were soundly defeated. Ed Streater was taken prisoner by the Confederates, one of 1,500 taken that day.

THOMAS TO MATTIE:

Buffalo July 24th 64

Dear Mattie

I have just recd another of you welcome Letters but had commenced to think you had forgotten there was any such person as my humble self. I am happy to hear that your health is so much better and hope it may continue so for I know now how to appreciate good health. I recd a letter from Lizzie a few days ago. I presume her name is Mrs Wanner ere this. I hope she may not repent of her bargain But Well the less said the sooner mended so I will keep still and wish Them a long life and a happy one. We are having Delightful weather here just now although it is rather dry. How I wish I was out there for just one week to travel over those Bluffs again it would be just the change I want now after being confined in the office so much, but it is of no use for me to think of it this Summer but I shall not say what I may do next although it is a long time to look ahead.

Mattie pack up your Trunk and come down here this fall. I know you would enjoy it very much and a change would do you good. Sarah and myself have a nice cosy little place here and I feel sure you could enjoy yourself if you would only come. We only live two or three streets from Mr Reeds and you know they would be just as glad to see you as we should so just pack up and come and make us a good long visit. I am not going to Prophesay any more in regard to the War for I must admit that I was mistaken about Richmond but still I do not feel at all Discouraged for my Confidence in Genl Grant is firm and unshaken. Genl Sherman is doing a Splendid work now and I hope ere long to hear of the Capture of Atlanta. Mattie I dont want you to think I am to hard on the South for I do not think I am. It is not my wish to hear of another gun being fired but the South brought on the War and until they say quit I say keep on if War is what they want give them enough to sicken them of it and I think now the only way to get a permanant Peace is to whip them and the sooner it is done the better.

Sarah is on the Lounge and fast asleep so I will not close this until she wakes up for I think she will want to enclose a line. Give my Kind Regards to Mary and accept the same Yourself. Write soon and

Believe me Your Friend
Thomas Townsend

Edgar Richmond in Uniform
Cairo, Illinois
Private collection of
Susan T. Puck

Back in Action

The enlistments of the men who volunteered in 1861 were up in 1864, and a draft was instituted to help fill the ranks. A county that could fill its quota with volunteers would not have men drafted, so there were bounties offered for enlistment which varied from state to state. The highest were to the men already in the army for their reenlistment, but all volunteers received some sort of bonus.

In spite of his miserable experience in the army hospital and in full knowledge of the casualties inflicted on the 23rd Wisconsin Volunteers, Ed Richmond reenlisted in Company C of the 42nd Regiment, Wisconsin Volunteers, which was mustered in on September 7, 1864. There were some familiar names in the regiment: Northrup, two Burlingames, and two Richmonds, as Ed's brother Dave enlisted with him. They moved to Cairo, Illinois, September 20 and remained there on post and garrison duty for the rest of the war, although detachments were sent out to other points in Illinois from time to time.

The following letter from Ed Richmond to Mary Van Ness shows that he could be quite eloquent when the occasion demanded it.

Ed to Mary:

Camp Randall Sept 15, 4o'clock /64

Dear Mary

I have at this moment received your kind letter which relieved me very much. I just as much expected to meet you once as I live. Yet such is disappointment. I have not time to write one minute as the drummer has already beat. I send you my Photograph such as it is, and hope I shall receive yours in return quickly.

Dear Mary here is a ring I expected to place upon your finger, but I cannot will you place it there remembering my love for you is as endless as this pledge.

If I had bid you good bye the other day I should feel a great deal better, but remember I think no less of you. If I could see you and talk with you once more I could go to Washington feeling well, but you know we cant calculate. Good Bye Dear Mary. Write often and remember your best friend on earth.

Ed

P.S. George wants to start and I must go Good Bye

Just exactly what Ed's gift of a ring to Mary meant to either of them is uncertain. He never mentions her in his succeeding letters, and Thomas does not say anything about her in his letters. If it were a true engagement, it seems likely that Mattie would have mentioned it in her letters to Thomas as he certainly enjoyed hearing about the romantic goings on of his friends back in Wisconsin.

Abraham Lincoln was up for reelection in the fall of 1864. His opponent was "Little Mac"—General George McClellan, whom Lincoln had replaced as commander of the Army of the Potomac with General Burnside and, ultimately, with General Grant.

The following letter was written by Ed Richmond to Ira Smith of West Point. It was discovered when Smith was going through some papers in 1899 and was printed by the Lodi *Enterprise* of March 10 of that year.

Cairo, Ill. Sept. 30, 1864

Friend Ira I take the opportunity to fulfill the promise I made to you about writing. It has been and is quite rainy and wet here, and we can't find a great deal to do only write letters and music. You have undoubtedly heard before this where we are, and now I will tell you what we are doing, and that is Post Duty. It is requisite that this place as well as others on the border should be guarded not only from the attacks of guerillas, which are both sides of us, but to keep quiet and peace in the surrounding country, and this 42nd regiment is stationed here for a while at least for that purpose. Some think we will stay here one year, and others not longer than spring. We have taken the place of the 139th Illinois three months men and they have returned home. Some of our boys are gone all the while up and down the river guarding prisoners, conscripts, deserters and bounty jumpers. William Rider and two or three other boys are on their way to Memphis now, guarding some deserters down, and that Dutchman that worked for Mitchell has just returned from there. His business was guarding prisoners. Stephen Lewis has gone to Louisville on some such duty, and so you can see about what is required of us. The boys like such business first rate.

Our colonel is appointed post commander. Captain Humphrey is appointed inspector general and ordinance officer. Henry Lamb is the colonel's clerk. Walter Lyman is clerk in the commissary's department. Charles Early is commander of the fort, consequently our company is not very largely represented at roll call as Dave is the regimental bass drummer and I am one of the principal musicians.

The health of the regiment is generally good. William Chrisler is in hospital but is well as ever now. Austin Chrisler was left sick in Madison.

The citizens here in Cairo are in for Mac all over. They have McClelland clubs established in every ward and hold their meetings regular every week. I also find that the soldiers will give the boy a larger vote than is expected. Company H stands half and half for old Abe and Little Mac. Now Uncle Ira, I must close by telling you I shall expect an answer next week with all the news and the prices of grain up there. Give my respects to Aunt Lucinda and Elwood and his wife. From Your friend, *Ed*

Ed Richmond's mother, Polly Richmond, was a widow, her husband Anson having died in 1856, the year after the family moved to Wisconsin. At the time of the next letter she was 58.

ED TO ADELINE:

Cairo Ill Oct 15 1864

Dear Sister

I have been waiting to get an answer from Ike before I wrote again but none had come and now I will write to you and see if you will do any better. Ike said in his letter to Dave as ye give so shall ye receive therefore he cant expect any more from me for I have not received what I have given.

To commence with I am well as common with the exception of a slight cold which I have catched in consequence of the change of weather. I have however just taked 3 of Ayers pills and if I receive one half the blessing that Hiram pronounced as I took them one by one I shall be prepared to jump any ten foot fence in the country by tomorrow morning.

Dave is getting along finely. He will come back to the barracks to morrow if nothing happens. I tell you the new bass drum needs a man that can beat it right. Hi has been to the Hospital for a few days, but is with us again now. Austin Chrisler has come, he is well.

Since I have been writing half of our regiment have been ordered to go on to the boat armed and equiped. I have this minute seen them march on our company is with them they expect to be gone two or three days near as I can get at it - they are going down the river about 25 miles to take some guerillas who are constantly fireing in to steam boats that are passing up and down the river not many of the musicians have gone.

I got a letter from Aunt Julia this afternoon. She says that Mort and herself are going home with Ma and that Uncle Dave is going to sell out and go to in the spring isnt that good news. I hope they will like it there. May be that Uncle would take my place if Ike has not let it-

I hear that Stephen Lewis is coming down here next month if so I would like to have you send me some things if he will fetch them. I would like a can of butter a piece of cheese, a little honey and a loaf of Indian bread. I can buy such things here but I cant get that that is good and sweet like yours. I will pay all expense. I played for a dance with John and Lewis last wednesday evening we played till 12 oclock and got 2 dollars apiece, they want us to play twice a week all winter if we stay here. we dont know whether we will or not yet.

George and Sarah in their letters asked me if I am fife Major tell them yes, and that Dave is Bass drummer. Beeby is Drum Major. I must stop for it is time to play the tattoo.

From your Brother Ed

Write soon. give my respects to all friends

The following is the last existing letter from Thomas to Mattie. She was visiting in Michigan and it was sent to her there. In Thomas's plea to her to visit him and Sarah, he says "now that you are so near us," but no matter where she was in Michigan, it would have more than doubled her travel distance if she had gone on to Buffalo as Thomas wanted her to do.

THOMAS TO MATTIE:

Oct 18th 1864

Dear Friend

Your kind favor of Oct. 5 is before me. Many many thanks of the same. I had thought myself entirely forgotten by friends in the West but am very happy to find it is not so. On one Condition I will freely forgive you. That is that you will not commit the Same Offence again. The Things you spoke of in your letter was all news to Me. Some Things Surprised me very much, More Especially Eds Enlisting again but I think if he has to go through as many hardships as the 23rd for the Next Year after he left he wont want to Enlist the Third time. Emmas and Jimmies affairs do not surprise me much for I was well enough acquainted with Emma to know that She was somewhat fickleminded. (Excuse me for speaking so plain of my Lady Friends) I rather Doubt whether Married Life brings Jimmie much Happiness. I am very sorry that you could not have arranged Things as to have paid us a visit now that you are so near us. It is to bad that you are not Coming. Cant you arrange it so as to come now; say, yes. I think you can if you try. If I could leave business and knew that you were not Coming I should surely try to come there and see you but it is Impossible for me to leave just at present as we are three Clerks Short in the Office here now and are very much Hurried. I have not seen Miss Reed since recd. your letter but will Give her your Message the first Opportunity. What kind of Weather are you having in Michigan. It is very unpleasant here. It rains nearly all the time, This Afternoon it is Snowing and is quite Cold. I had not heard a word from Mr. Bartholomews folks Since Lizzies Marriage until I read your letter. Lizzie write me just before the Happy day and that is the last I had heard from them so you see my western news has been very Limited.

Well Mattie what do you think of the War now, do you not see that it is nearly at an end. I think I can almost see the End. Lincoln will be reelected and then the Rebels will see that there is still Power at the North. I hope it will be settled soon but in no other way than for the South to return to there allegiance so that we may have a United Government. I care not for Slavery. Although I do think Slavery was the Cause of all this Bloodshed. Some have told me that I fought for the Nigger. *No Never.* I fought to help put down the Rebellion and if by so doing I did help to Free the Nigger I am not to blame. I believe in Weakening the Rebels in every way we can and if it can be done best by taking there Property I say take it be it Nigger or be it Mules, but instead of a friendly letter I am writing a political one so enough of that. I will try and finish this to Morrow.

Sunday afternoon

You wished to know whether we had heard any thing of Edward Streater we have only heard from him once since his Capture and that was a long time age we feel very anxious about him. Do you keep a Record of the Co as you thought you would. I should like to see it very much. Then I should like to take a trip to Wis. I know I should Enjoy myself so well. I often think of the time I was there and think of it as the happiest year and a half of my life had it not been for the Skirmish with Mr. Raynolds Trouble and me would have been Strangers in that time.

Sunday Evening Sarah and Myself have just returned from Church and I dont know but I am wicked in sitting right down to writing but I Cant help it. I know I am wicked and who is not. Let him that Sin not cast the first Stone. Do You intend Teaching again this Winter or have you taught enough. I intend to try and have Sarah quit it this winter for she is killing herself by keeping on. I know it must be a very tedious job to be confined all day in a house with so many Children.

Now Mattie do come and see us if possible and if it isnt possible make it possible and come any way. I think I have written as much as you will want to read so will stop. Hoping this will find you well and enjoying yourself as I have no Doubt you are. Remember me to all enquiring Friends in Wisconsin Give my kind Regards to Mary and believe me as ever Your Sincere Friend

Thomas Townsend
My address is Box 2328
Buffalo
NY

Sarah says do not seal it I will write Mattie to Morrow Please excuse all Mistakes from your

Friend Thomas

The War Ends

General Robert E. Lee surrendered his Army of Virginia on April 9, 1865, but the war was not quite over.

EDGAR TO ISAAC:

Cairo Ill May 1st 1865

Dear Brother

I received your letter in due time.

We are all well as usual with one or two exceptions. Harvey Barnes is in the Hospital sick with the Lung fever I believe, it was an accute attack, & he is getting better fast, he thinks will be out in a week or so. George Mortor is in there too with sore eyes. He has been quite sick otherwise.

Hi Northrup has had the mumps but is better or I should say well & doing duty. Den York is sick with them now, I hope he wont catch cold, with the few exceptions Co C is all right.

Our Reg is all here now except Co B who are at Springfield Ill., there is also two companies of Ill troops here under the command of our Colonel, making eleven companies, the boys are having it much easier now. The boys are all feeling good over the probability of being sent home in a short time, I suppose you have seen the order to reduce the expenses of the Government one million dollars a day, & reduce the number of men in the army to four hundred thousand. If we are one of the lucky Reg you can look for us in a month or so if not, then we shall stay until our time is out, which not a very long time at the longest. There is all manner of speculation in regard to it here among the boys, & nothing else talked of at present.

Well if we stay I am having a very soft thing just now for a soldier, since Co H came back & drove us out of their barracks & broke up our Mess, the Drum Major & I have been boarding with the rest of Non Commish at the Soldiers Home, all Soldiers who have no companies to fall back on can board there, all we have to do is go about 30 rods on a good walk, & eat, & have good living. I find it is no disadvantage to have an office even if it is a small one like mine.

Earley says he had a good visit with you think you have two very smart children & your wife, well I shant say what he said about her but thinks it is the place for him & his wife to visit. The weather has been quite chilly for a day or two the river is going down fast. Write soon of course

Ed

Although General Robert E. Lee surrendered to General Grant on April 9, 1865, it was May 26 before the Confederate forces in the Mississippi area, led by General E. Kirby Smith, surrendered. On May 27 Ed Streater was released from Confederate prison at Red River Landing, Louisiana. In the two years and ten months he was in the army he had survived typhoid fever, fought in and around the swamps of Mississippi and Louisiana for a year and a half and spent a year as a prisoner of war. When he was mustered out in Madison, Wisconsin, on June 21, he was 21 years old.

The 23rd Regiment, Wisconsin Volunteers, was mustered out on July 4, 1865, two years to the day after Vicksburg fell. The regiment lost one officer and 40 enlisted men killed and mortally wounded during service and five officers and 262 enlisted men from disease, for a total of 308 or about 30 percent of the regiment. These figures do not take into account the men who were wounded and survived or those like Ed, Gib, and Thomas who were discharged because of illness.

When the news that the war was over reached the 42rd Regiment, Ed Richmond was so excited that he dented his fife when he hit it on a post while waving it in the air. The regiment was discharged on the twentieth of June, 1865. During the nine and a half months it was in service, no men were killed or mortally wounded but 58 were lost from disease.

Ed Richmond and Mary Van Ness were married September 16. In the 1870s he built a house on a hill in Lodi which was home to the family for the next eighty years. They had two girls, Mary Emma and Grace, and two boys, George and Albert. Albert's children were Laurence and Jessie June, the only grandchildren of Ed and Mary to reach adulthood.

Mary Van Ness Richmond, circa 1900
Private collection of Susan T. Puck

Edgar Richmond, circa 1900
Private collection of Susan T. Puck

In 1883 Ed applied for and received a pension of $42.27 a month on the grounds that his health had been permanently damaged by the "bronchitis and shortness of breath" he had as a result of his experience on the trip from Louisville to Memphis in November 1862. Sworn statements from former Lt. Robert Steele, Ira Smith, and Dr. E. Howard Irwin were presented as confirmation of his testimony. Since one attack of bronchitis can leave a person more susceptible to future attacks and severe attacks can damage the lungs, Ed's problem undoubtedly did stem from his first enlistment even though he was well enough to reenlist in 1864.

Ed was one of the founders of the Lodi *Enterprise*, a newspaper which is still being published, and was running a general store at the time of his death in 1903. Mary and her daughters continued to run it for several years after that. The fixtures from the store and Ed's silver fife were donated to the State Historical Society of Wisconsin in Madison after the deaths of his children.

Epilogue

In 1912 the Postmaster at Lodi received the following letter:

Norfolk Va Mch4/12
P.M. Lodi Wis

Dear Sir

Please pardon me for troubling you in this way, but I wish to get some information thru you. At the Breaking out of the Civil War I was in the employ of Milton Bartholomew a short distance from your village, and enlisted from there in the 23rd Wis Regiment, Co. H. I wish to know if any of that Co are still living in or near Lodi, and if so who are they. Is Lieut Steele still alive. There was a family by the name of Van Ness living on the road between Lodi and Sauk. In the family were two sons and two daughters. The Daughters names were Martha and Mary. During the little unpleasantness I sent to Martha a roster of our com H. Is she still living, if so can you furnish me with her address as I should like very much to get a copy of the roster. Would like very much to hear from some of the boys if any There are in that section. Thanking you for any information you may be able to furnish me.

I am yours truly
Thos Townsend
118 No. Park ave,
Norfolk Va

The Postmaster passed the letter on to Mary Van Ness Richmond.

THOMAS TO MARY:

Norfolk Va March 11th 12

Dear Friend

Your very kind letter of the 9th to hand and I certainly want to thank you for the kind interest you take in one of whom you knew so little. Life is not long enough for me to ever forget the many pleasant afternoons I spent at your home and the many kindnesses shown to the strange boy in a strange land by both you and your Dear Sister Martha, whom at that time I loved with all the ardor of the boy just arriving at manhood and felt that life would not be worth living without her. I well remember the letter I wrote her from Vicksburg in regard to the passing away of one of the best of men. It was the hardest task ever impressed on me knowing the situation as I did and the sadness it must give to that loving heart. I can only see Martha and you as you then were. I can easily realize that I am an old man of 73 years and a grandfather but you two are so firmly fixed in memory that I assure you I feel that you must still be the girls down at the old homestead.

Now to answer some of your questions in regard to myself. After the war I returned to Buffalo and as soon as I was able to work got a position in the Buffalo P.O. was there several years Then was offered a fine position as shipping clerk in the American Express Co. In the meantime had taken unto myself a wife. In the summer of 1869 the company saw fit to cut the salarys of their Employes. I at once tendered my resignation and started once more for the west to the then growing state of Kansas, leaving my wife and one child with her parents. She was an only child. In the spring of 70 they all packed up and came to me at Irving Marshall Co Kansas.

We spent 10 years and a half there and prospered so far as property and finance went but my Dear Wifes health failed and the Dr. said I must take her East to or near the Sea Shore, so sacrificed my land and stock and came here to Norfolk where her health improved, and she was with me and we were one, until one year ago last October. Together for 45 years and happy, but now what a lonely old man only waiting for time that we may again be together if only in spirit. We were blessed with three children our oldest a girl born in Buffalo. The other two a boy and girl born in the sunflower state. The oldest Daughter we laid to rest 12 years ago, the other two are living. My home is with my Daughter who has a son a boy of six years, an unusually bright boy who thinks no prank to bad to put on his grandfather. My Son has one boy nearly 18 years of age. On arriving here thirty one years ago I went into a Rental and Real Estate business in which in the parlance of the day I made good and became comfortably well off. It is quite warm here in the summer and for twenty years before losing my Wife we spent our Summers in the northern mountains of New York Vt and New Hampshire. During our stay on a Lake near the White Mts of N.H. many Years ago I met a former Captain of one of the Companys of the 23 Wis. He was formerly a member of our Co.H but was promoted to Capt of another Co. A Captain Baker. We spent one day together at Lake Winnepsauge at the camp where the old vets of NH meet each summer, and such a day. Ladys have the credit of being great talkers but if any two of them could have done more of it than we did that day they deserve all the credit we could give them. For the last six years of Dear Wifes life she was a great sufferer from that dread trouble cancer. Five years ago I retired from business in order that I might devote my time to her. We spent a good portion of three years in Buffalo with a specialist, but money, time, love and devotion could not cure her and she went to her rest a year ago Last October. I have here at my home a very large lot and it was my wifes pleasure to fill that with flowers, more especially roses of which she has some 50 different varieties. I spend a great deal of my time now taking care of and working amongst them, and in their pleasant blooming way they talk to me of her who was so fond of them, they bloom with us here from May to January it seems to be their natural home.

Now a word in regard to Martha. I do wish I had known she was in Lincoln Neb. for so many years. We had a very close friend there. He was Clerk of the Court there and also State Librarian for many years. His wife was a celebrated singer and once when in Europe she sang for Queen Victoria. His name was David Campbell. I have not heard from him now for several years and think he left there and went to Denver Col near which place he had a large sheep ranche. In Kansas City I had a sister living until about two years ago who is now at Corpus Christi Texas for her health. She visited me in Wis when I was with Mr. Bartholomew. I should loved to have had them meet each other.

You will find on the Co roll the name of Seth Tannehill. He came down to Buffalo in the late sixties and studied telegraphy and was often in our home. Do you know any thing of him. So Mary Reed is still living. She must be of a ripe old age. I left Buffalo with them and traveled with them to Lodi, Please give her my Love and much kind Regards. Tell her that my Wife was an old friend of hers and used to be a visiter at her home when she lived out near the Fair

Grounds. Her maiden name was Hattie A Day. If her memory has not failed too much I am sure she will remember her. I am very much pleased to know that your life has been a happy one and that you are blessed in your children and grandchildren and can also sympathise with you in the loss of your helpmeet. I devote right much of my time to my church work, have been Senior Warden of the Episcopal Church for a great many years. I love the work and it helps to keep my mind employed now that I am out of business. If not asking too much of you I certainly would love to have a copy of the Co H Roster of the old 23rd. I used often to see your late or ex Senator Vilas a gentleman of the first water when he was in Washington both when PostMaster Genl and also when Senator and he was always pleased to see any of the old 23rd boys. Has your home town of Lodi grown much since those stormy days.

The rest of this letter is missing

What Thomas did not tell Mary, unless it was included in the missing portion of his letter, was what happened when he applied for a pension in August of 1884. He must have been horrified when the pension office notified him that he was listed as a deserter on the Company roll from October 1863 through February 1864. It took him until July 6, 1887, to get the charges removed.

Mary Van Ness Richmond died March 13, 1913, after a long illness. She was not quite seventy years old. The following letter exists as a handwritten copy in her daughter Mary Emma's hand. The original was probably sent to Mattie in California.

Norfolk Va. - March 24th -13

To the children of my Boyhood Friend
Dear Friends

Your village paper to hand this A.M. and with Sorrow and grief in my own heart I wish to express to you my deepest sympathy in this your great affliction. The loss of a good and Loving Mother. Who is it that can fill or take her place. Who is it that can make such sacrifices as only a devoted mother will make for the children she so dearly loves. I can most deeply sympathise with you in your loss, for I too only two short years ago was called upon to pass through the deep waters of affliction in the loss of a Dear and

Loving Wife after forty five years of happy union together. As she has probably told you, It was my good fortune to know her over fifty years ago, when but a boy, and a stranger in a strange land and of the kindness then bestowed upon that wandering way ward boy by both your mother and her sister are some of the bright spots in my memory that Father Time has not managed to efface. Then let us try to realize that she is not dead but sleepeth and is waiting your coming on the other shore. With grief mingled with your grief.

I remain your mothers Friend
Thos Townsend

Thomas Townsend had to wait another nine years before he could join his wife "if only in spirit." He died in March 1922, at the age of eighty-three.

Martha (Mattie) Van Ness never married. Sometime after 1871 she moved to Lincoln, Nebraska, where she lived for many years. In 1907 she made a trip to California to visit friends in Clovis and Long Beach, and after making another trip there, she sold her house in Lincoln in 1912 and moved to Santa Ana, California, at the age of seventy-three. She died in the county hospital, Orange County, California, on August 25, 1919, at the age of eighty.

A letter from her friend Lucinda Gardner to "The Richmond Family" at the time of her death tells of Mattie's long interest in her church and especially the missionary society and ends with,

---

I think our life together was full of pleasant things in connection with missions and church work and I am sorry her last years were not more with her Lodi friends, we would all have enjoyed it very much. But her heart was in Calif and she could not leave it, and also with missions, to the last, but her mind failed her and she died in the Hospital. Heaven is as near California as in Wisconsin.

She might have also included Virginia, Massachusetts, and Vicksburg, Mississippi.

Appendix

Letters of Brainerd Cummings to Mary Van Ness

Thomas Townsend and Will Shurtleff were not the only people who corresponded with the Van Ness women during the war. Since writing letters was the only way people could keep in touch, it was a popular pastime. Mattie carried on a regular correspondence with Thomas's sister Sarah, and Mary Van Ness wrote to a former boarder in her father's house, Sgt. Brainerd Cummings, from the time he left Winconsin in 1859 to the end of 1864.

Brainerd Cummings, 30, was native of Maine, but he spent the school year of 1858-1859 in Wisconsin, where he was a teacher in the West Point school. Whether Mary was his student is not known, but since he lived in the Van Ness household, he knew the family well and wrote to Mary and other West Point friends, including Will Shurtleff, after he left Wisconsin and returned to his family in Massachusetts. He enlisted in Company A, 7th Regiment, New Hampshire Volunteer infantry in 1861. The only letter that exists from the period before the war is given here as an introduction to him and his rather scholarly style.

Andover, May 2nd, 1859

Mon Ami: Mary

Will you pardon me for the liberty I have taken in writing to you without first asking permission to do so?

I might have said when I was in West Point, with your permission I will write to you, but although I did not do so I have ventured to inflict a letter upon you, having a good opinion of your good nature.

About that Phillipena (I do not know as I spell the name correctly)[11] I supose that ere this you have received a book from me which I hope may prove interesting and worth reading. Please accept as a friend and teacher's token of respect and esteem. I think I about spoiled the presentation plate by scrawling my name and yours on it with some of my usual blunders. I am very sorry for it and most sincerely hope you will erase it or keep it out of sight. It is almost comtemptable for any gentleman to do so badly, and I have felt ashamed and nearly mad every time I have thought of it. I suppose it wouldn"t have looked like me if it had been written well. But enough of this.

The 9 o'clock bell is ringing a good night deary and pleasant dreams and tomorrow night I will see if my dull brain will bring forth something more.

May 3

Again I have gotten into my room in a rather poor boarding house alone and time will tell show what I will get on to my paper tonight.

I am residing in the old puritanical town of Andover of which I will attempt some discription.

It is one of the old and beautiful towns of Mass. It is a very quiet and moral town and a first rate place for a youth of steady habits.

The village in which I reside is quite large and one of the prettiest places I ever saw. Most of the residences are large and good and many of them may be called splendid. The streets and walks are shaded by magnificent Elms, Maples, and Horse Chestnuts, which are now just beginning to put forth their leaves.

The town is noted for its literary and theological institutions, superannuated ministers and old maids. There are any quantity of the latter here, and I do not know why it is, unless they wait for a minister until it is too late to get any decent man. The institutions of the place are the Theo. semanary, Phillip's Acadamy, Abbot Female Semanary and Punchard free school.

This is a grand place for a rich man and perhaps about as good as any place for a poor man. It's great attraction for me is two brothers and two sisters and $1.50 per day check.

There is very little going on here by way of amusement but they manage to have sewing[12] circles occasionally some of which are pretty good. I have been to three since I have been here and that is all I have had in the way of fun. I should be happy to take a good horse and carriage (we have such here, and good roads) and drive round with you some two weeks hence when spring shall have put on her most beautiful robe.

I intended to get out to Fox Lake before I left Wis. but I began to grow homesick pretty soon after my school closed and as I was idle I got off soon as possible.

How did you and Aunt Libby get along the last term?

I have the honor to be slightly acquainted with Miss Nellie T. Jand. She is rather squashy and fat but a perfect brick.

I think you will find her pretty good company if you throw aside all feelings of dislike for the Lodi people and all preconceived notions respecting her if you have any. Give her all credit for all good there is about her and overlook her faults. Please give my respects to her.

A few words to Martha. I am under obligation to you for that note though I could wish it had been longer. However the smallest favors thankfully received and larger ones in proportion. I burned the note as you desired.

I do not know but it will do for me to flatter myself that I did awaken some slight feeling of regard among the people (some of them) out West and I should be sorry were it otherwise.

I am pretty reckless but I should hate very much to be disliked by everybody. I wish it might be practicable for me to visit Wis. and see you all again but I hardly think I ever can do so. Please bear in mind that I shall ever entertain feelings of true regard for "Mary and her sister Martha" and I should be happy to hear from them often.

Tell Isaac that I will answer his letter soon.

Please give my respects to the other members of the family and I will not afflict you with any more of my hurried chirography[13] at present.

Yours truly
Brainerd Cummings

P.S. I am very willing to receive the title of adopted brother. B.C.

After his enlistment in 1861, Brainerd Cummings was stationed on the East coast. He was in Florida when he wrote the first wartime letter to Mary that still exists.

BRAINERD TO MARY:

St. Augustine, Fla. March 21st, 1863

Friend Mary,

I received your very interesting letter of March 1st a few days since, and this is the first chance I have had to answer it. It seems to have been warm during the winter nearly all over the county, but I understand that they are having a cold March North with more snow now than they have had during the winter. Perhaps it has been so with you. Here we have had considerable wet, but it has not been cold even for this place. I have seen no ice this winter, and but little frost, yet such is the change here and the warmth of some of the winter days that we feel the cold days almost as much as we do in Maine. Those that have done duty in the open air here had to be pretty warmly clothed, and had to keep stiring to keep comfortable. I like the winter here very well, how I shall like the summer in this town remains to be seen. I liked being in Fort Jefferson very well, as the sea breezes made it very comfortable there. I have spent a summer and winter in the south and it has passed away very rapidly and comfortably, and there is a chance of our having to pass another summer and winter here. I hope not but if it is to be so I shall try to take the matter easy. I hardly know whether I should call Ed. and Gilbert fortunate or unfortunate. They were fortunate in getting discharged when out of health. I should however rather have my health and stay in the service until the war was over.

When I was at Lodi I knew George Kingsley though he was just a boy then. He was a sweet goodhearted fellow.

It is the fortune of war to have many of the best killed and we have to submit. I should judge that Mattie might be having a good chance at Lodi, and I think you have a pretty good chance what there is of it. You can too, have a chance to entertain that sick soldier. I think it would suit me very well to have you there teaching if I was in Gilbert's place. I hope he will get entirely well. This would be a good place for him. This climate would cure him of the bronchitis. This is one of the most healthy place in the world they say here, and I am willing to agree with them.

Yes, I am 30 and a little more though I feel just about as I did when I was in Wis. I do not know how it is with girls after they are 25, but I do not think they grow worse after that age, unless they are very anxious to get married. If that is the case they are a little apt to show it and excite other feelings in persons than those of perfect respect. I hardly think you will grow old any faster after you are 25 than before, if you do not get married but I suppose you are pretty sure of getting married. Well I hope you will get one of the best men that ever lived, and he may think himself fortunate. We are having a time here now that is not so very pleasant for us. Last Friday a transport came in bringing orders for the departure of one half of this Regt. and — seventy-five companies with the bal. left this town yesterday for Hilton Head. I suppose they are determined to cooperate in an attack upon Charleston or Savannah.

The companies took 25 days rations with them and took no extra clothing, nor no camp equippage that they could get along without for a few weeks. The movement meens work, and the 7th Regt. may have a chance to show themselves.

There is too a "right smart chance" for an attack on this place in the absense of the five companies for we have quarter-master's and commissary stores enough to make it something of a temptation to attack it. However if an army of one or two thousand men undertake to get the place we can in this old fort make it rather dangerous work for them. My Capt. told me tonight that he thought there was much more than an even chance of an attack. Let them come if they wish to. Many of the soldiers that have left had made warm friends here, and there were some tears shed by the natives when they left. One of them has got married. I cannot say much for his taste however for his wife is a very imperious looking woman and too young to get married. I think they were both very foolish. The Regt. has many friends here and is popular. The people are certainly used very well and they use us well. I can hardly tell you who my nearest friend is in the company. One that I am quite intimate with is a Sergeant about my size 37 years old, dark hair and eyes, and whiskers and has had two wives. The man that I liked best of any in the Co. died at Beaufort last summer. His name was Charles Stevens. He was just a little larger than I am and looked some like me, so much so that one was mistaken for the other by strangers sometimes. You would have liked him first rate. He was social and gentlemanly and was made a sergeant just before he died. The man that I have the highest respect for in the company is a hospital attendent. He is good looking, has a full black beard, and of good hight and form. He is married and has two very pretty children. Some of our best men have died.

The next time that I write I hope that I can say that there has been something done in this department and I hope that Charleston and Savannah will soon be taken. There is now a very large fleet and a large body of troops in the vicinity of Hilton Head, and I think they will give a good account of themselves. My health continues to be good, though I am troubled with sore eyes a little at this time. Give my regards to all the friends in West Point and Lodi. Please write as often as you can.

Yours truly,
Brainerd Cummings

Thomas Townsend's brother was not the only soldier in trouble in the assault on Fort Wagner in the summer of 1863. The 7th New Hampshire Regiment was sent from Florida to Morris Island, South Carolina, and six days after the fall of Vicksburg they took part in the bloody Fort Wagner assaults of July 10, 11, and 18. Sergeant Brainerd Cummings was hit by a bullet on the 18th.

By this time Brainerd and Mary Van Ness had been corresponding for four years without having seen each other since he had left West Point, Wisconsin, in April of 1859, when she was sixteen and he was twenty-six.

BRAINERD TO MARY:

U. S. Gen Hospital, Fort Schyler, n.y. Sept.22,63

My Dear Friend,

I received a letter that you sent to Port Royal after I had been here some weeks, but having written to you from here, I have waited for another letter from you before I wrote again, But I have waited in vain, and now I am commencing another letter to you in the hope that it will get an answer.

I was pained to hear of the death of William Shurtleff. I thought him a man in the highest sense of the term, and he must have been respected by his company if they had been decent.

I pity his family — it was a very severe loss to them. So it goes, this war is taking of a large number of the best of men who it seems might otherwise live to be an ornament to society and of great use in the world. Yet I see no other way but to fight this war out to the bitter end, at whatever cost. So the bell that I left is still doing duty in the schoolroom. Its peal was promptly answered when I used it and I presume it is so now.

I think I look very much as I did when you last saw me, though I suppose I have grown old some and perhaps you might say a great deal. I have now been in the hospital a little more than two months and during that time I have been reading the news, novels, and cultivating side whiskers and a moustache. However I cannot say that I have succeeded in raising "a perfect love of a moustache" for it is still small. I got it started when I was on Morris Island, and the first two or three weeks in the hospital when I had but little opportunity to get shaved, and afterward I thought I would let it grow and see what it would come to.

I should hope that the marriages do not cause much roughness in the movements of society in West Point, if deaths do. The latter are usually melancholy to be sure, and particularly so in such cases as that mentioned. I knew Mr. Ransford and family well. I do not see what made you think I was a "confirmed old bach." I certainly was not very old when you used to see me, much as I feel myself very old now, though a little more than thirty.

You seem to have changed your mind, and write as though you thought I had someone in view whom I expected to make Mrs. Cummings. I do not understand why you jump at that conclusion either, Have you seen any reason to change your mind? I do not think I ever gave you good folks in West Point any cause to call me a woman hater, and I think I have been accused of being smitten with the charms of a certain "Assemblyman's daughter" though that was never the case with me, and now you say you thought me a confirmed bach. Now I always had the vanity to think that I could get married sometime, although I certainly never felt in a hurry to do so, nor did I ever fancy that I was a favorite among the ladies and I yet hope to marry a girl that is good looking and amiable, all in good time. When I do it I will send you my card, and further particulars. But if as you seem to think I am partly engaged to someone do you think she would be willing to have me send you my photograph? Well I will see about that when I get a chance to get it taken and if you answer this letter promptly perhaps I will. It is possible that you have not received my last letter, and I will just say that I was wounded in a charge on Fort Wagner July 18th, through the right arm, right side, and left thumb shot away. I was a week in the hospital at Beauford, S.C. when I was sent here, where I have been slowly getting well. My arm and thumb are healed, but the wound in my side is still open and still very sore. About a week since a small piece of bone came out of it, and I presume there are more to come out, enough to keep it sore. I have not been off the hospital grounds yet though I have been all the time able to move about a little.

I wish it had been my fortune to pass through the siege of Charleston before getting disabled, but it was not and I must submit. My general health is excellent and has been ever since the Regt went on to Morris Island July 10th.

I hope I get a letter from you soon. I certainly shall if you want that Photograph much.

Please give my regards to the good friends in West Point, particularly the members of your family.

I most sincerely hope your parents will live many years yet in health and the enjoyment of a green old age. My father died a week ago today.

Yours truly,
Brainerd Cummings
U. S. Gen Hospital, Ward 12, Sec. C
Fort Schyler, N.Y.

If a soldier had a wound like Brainerd's now, the physician would probably surgically remove the pieces of bone that were shattered. However, during the Civil War it was safer to let the wound heal by itself than to operate. Sterile techniques were totally unknown, and it was rare that a doctor would even rinse off his instruments from one patient to the next, let alone wash his hands. Recovery from infection of any kind depended on the patient's own recuperative powers.

BRAINERD TO MARY:

U. S. General Hospital
Fort Schyler,New York Sept. 28th 1863

Friend Mary,

I received your letter of Sept. 23rd was very gladly received today and after reading it I turned immediately round in my chair to answer it.

I wrote to you just a week ago and I hope you have got the letter ere this time, and I hope you will not write until you have received this and then we can go on regular with our writing if it suits you.

I did get a pretty close shot at Fort Wagner and I have not got over it yet, and today the prospect of soon getting well is not very flattering. I believe I have been rather growing worse for the last week, as far as that wound in the side goes, and today I am suffering considerable pain from it, and it feels as though it was swollen around the place where the ball entered. I suspect there is some pieces of bone in the wound yet that have got to come out or some other substance that should not be there. I hope things will come to a crisis with it soon.

I should enjoy an armchair in your house very much and I presume I could talk some but I could not say much about "Moving accidents by flood and field, Of hairbreadth scapes in the imminent deadly breach" for my soldier's life has been very tame, and I have seen but little adventure. I had just begun that kind of life when I was wounded. If I could have passed through the siege to the taking of Charleston I believe I could have willingly lost a leg. Certainly that would have been preferable to getting wounded at the outset as I did.

Congratulations on getting fine apples raised at home, and I agree with you that the West is a glorious country. I always thought so, though I did not fall in love with the country exactly.

Then your experience as a teacher is not very pleasant. I know there is much that is disagreeable and trying to ones patience about it, and there is something connected with it very pleasant to me. I am certainly glad that I have been a pedagogue. You can more see the reason for sour and fretful looks on my countenance, which I think you have often seen. I think I will send the Photograph when I can get it taken. It tires me considerable to write to day or I would write more. I hope John S. Cummings' family will be some think decent, but if they are so it will be in spite of a bad father. Remember me to friends in West Point. The sooner and longer you write the better it will suit me.

Yours truly,
Brainerd Cummings

When Brainerd Cummings said, "Moving accidents by flood and field, Of hairbreadth scapes in the imminent deadly breach," he was quoting from Shakespeare's *Othello*, Act 1, Scene 3. In this scene Othello is describing how he won Desdemona's heart by telling her father, in her hearing, about his military exploits. He ends by saying, "She loved me for the dangers I had passed, And I loved her that she did pity them." Mary was certainly familiar with the play, and the reference was not lost on her.

John S. Cummings was a resident of West Point, but his relationship to Brainerd is unknown. Brainerd's father's name was Francis.

Several of the letters from Thomas and Brainerd mention Jimmy and Em. They were James Richmond, Ed's cousin, and Emma Van Ness, a cousin of Mary and Mattie. Jimmy and Em were married on January 28, 1864.

In the following letter Brainerd Cummings says he thought James Richmond married Phil. Burlingame's daughter. He had his Richmonds mixed up as it was Ed's brother Dave who had married Maria Louisa Burlingame.

BRAINERD TO MARY:

Fort Wood, Bedloe's Island
New York Harbor Feb. 16th 1864

Friend Mary

Your very interesting letter of Feb. 1st reached me just as I was starting for the city, one object in going to get some Photographs taken. The said Photographs were finished and reached me yesterday, and I will enclose one in this letter. I do not like the picture very much for I had on an invalid uniform, the only one I have now, which is all light blue, which takes just no color at all. The pictures are all dark and it seems to me that the eyes are small. However I am not blessed with a pair of large, brilliant dark eyes. I do not know when I shall be able to get any other taken so I will send this, and perhaps I can sometime send a better one. I will now venture to make a proposition. I would like a representation of you of some kind very well, and if you will send me one, I will send you another, the best I can get in citizen's dress, and if any of the young ladies must take the advantage of the year, [Leap Year] and get me ensnared during the year, I will send you a photograph of my wife. I think that is fair and generous. I know your curiosity will make you wish to see how my wife looks, and as men out of the army are scarce it is not impossible that I may become a victim to the blandishments of some fair virgin that wishes to enter the state of matrimony.

So you play governess at Mr. Reynolds, and while you are playing governess, do you play any of your arts on Gilbert? How my scholars are getting ahead of their teacher, particularly in getting married. Well I do think of it, but I do not know as it makes me feel very sad. I most sincerely hope they will all enjoy themselves much better for being married, as no doubt they will. The latter marriage I should not have expected. Somehow I got it into my head that James Richmond married Phil. Burlingame's daughter. How was it? Was not that the intention at one time? You never told me about Burlingame's skedaddle. I used to think that some of the Van Ness family were rather severe on Phil, but I guess they must have been about right. We have had but very little snow here this winter, not more than six inches at a time, and not so much as that but once. It has been quiet most of the time, though we have had some pretty rough weather.

I am glad to learn that Lysander is doing well.

It is leap year sure enough, and you wish to show your power and nearly break the hearts of some honest swain. Well how fortunate it is that I am not in West Point. You might try to practice on me, just for the practice of course, and I am a little susceptable yet. Be merciful at least and write your name as Mrs.- Something before the year is out if you can.

I have very little of interest to write about here. I am now doing duty out of the company and acting as sort of commisssary sergeant for the convalescents. I have to look after the rations for about 500 now. I spent quite a pleasant day and evening in New York a week ago in attending Wm. Amburg's Managarie and Wallachs Theatre. My health is pretty good though just now I have a severe cold and cough.

Please give my congratulations to the newly married couples and my respects to all the friends in West Point and Lodi. I suppose Mr.—

I got as far as Mr. in some sentence when I was interupted,— Ah! I have just thought what I was going to write and will begin again.

I suppose Mr. Reynolds girls are nearly young ladies now if not quite. I should like to visit West Point again. Please write soon.

Yours truly, B. Cummings
Segt. Co.E. 21st Regt. USIC

At the end of this letter Brainerd Cummings signed himself as being in the 21st Regt. USIC, which stood for U.S. Invalid Corps. The Corps was made up of men who were not fit for full military service but who could still perform such limited work as guard and clerical duties. This freed many able-bodied men to fight. Unfortunately, the initials I-C also stood for "Inspected-Condemned" and were stamped on worn-out army equipment and mules. The name of the Invalid Corps was changed to the Veterans Reserve Corps in March 1864, and Brainerd uses this address in his next letter.[14]

BRAINERD TO MARY:

Fort Wood, New York Harbor
June 8th 1864

Friend Mary

Owing to my absence from this post for a few days, and the carelessness of the P.M. after I got back I did not get your letter of May 10th until last night. But if the getting it was long delayed, it was exceedingly welcome, though almost unexpected.

I had began to fear that you had taken offence at my joking, though I could hardly think that of you, or something else had happened to break off our intercourse, though you did not wait so very long after all.

Jokes, I am aware, sometimes give offence unless the parties understand each other thoroughly, and hence I think I think it is about as safe and pleasant not to make a practice of joking very much. I rather thought you and I understood each other so very well that we could take a joke, and I know by experience that you can give one.

Although I never expect to see Wis. again or any of the acquaintances I made there, it is very pleasant to feel that I have friends there, and I certainly would wish to retain them as long as possible. I shall always hold in remembrance the pleasant time I had in West Point, and I have been very glad to get your letters, particularly so since I have been in the army, and I would go far to meet you all again, though that can hardly be. I shall not take offence at anything that you may write, for I never saw any propensity in you to try to wound the feelings of any one, but thought you like a harmless joke.

But to explain the reason of my not getting your letter sooner.

The 17th of May, just before your letter reached here, I went to Mass. on a furlough of 15 days, and when I got back the P.M. neglected to give me your letter with others that had come for me in my absence, and he did not come across it until last night. I felt vexed to be kept out of a good letter for so long, but it was of no use to fret.

I had a very pleasant time during my stay at home, or at Andover, the place I call home now, and had the pleasure of meeting all my own brothers, and my oldest sister who is married and resides in Maine near our old home. She was quite unexpectedly at Andover on a visit while I was there. My unmarried sister was keeping house for the married one, and she has been with her for the last nine months nearly. She left her situation as teacher in an acadamy on account of father's sickness last summer, and as my oldest sister has had much sickness in her family she has stayed with her since father's death. It is misfortune to her in some respects to be kept from teaching but she would hardly be contented away from our oldest sister now with so much sickness in the family.

I should like very much to see those children and no doubt they are smart. I think that of my nieces and nephew, and I think as much of them I presume as you do of yours even if I am "a confirmed old Bach," I expect Isaac enjoys himself about as much as it is possible for one to on this earth. Well he has a right to, and I would if I was in his situation.

You have all been fortunate in being able to keep together. There has been no breaking up in your family. With me and the rest of the family it is quite different. I have always got homesick whenever I have tried to stay at home since the older members of the family left. I can appreciate the pleasure you derive from being all together. So Mattie is teaching in her own district rather a hard place, yet doubtless she will succeed to her own and others satisfaction. Miss Altelia Bush has got the start of you and Mattie, though I should hardly suppose she had got a very smart man, though I can not judge much by what I saw of him.

Western people are cases to get married, and I am almost surprised that you are yet single. I do not believe after all that you have said that the Misses Van Ness are very much more of the marrying kind than their humble servant, B.C. Leap year is nearly half gone.

We at the north hope that this summer will nearly end the war though some think it will continue several years longer yet. I most earnestly hope it will not, and there are none that long for this war to close more than the thinking soldiers.

They and their immediate friends are the greatest sufferers. Everybody has great confidence in Grant, and there is no jealousy because he is a Western man. He is the only man that would fight that army as it is fought, though we must not over look the merit of his commanders.

Hancock and Warren are hosts in themselves and without the cooperation of such men Grant could do nothing. Three years of fighting brings out the right men, and it is only continued struggles that can bring out the great leaders. I do not care where they come from, though I confess I take a more lively interest in men from my native state, and she, as well as the rest of N.E., has furnished her share of the noble men who have been leaders, and have finished in this war, and the West is indebted to N.E. for some of her brilliant men.

All have done too well to make comparisons. I have read quite a number of Scott's works and have found them all very interesting. Dickens I do not like quite as well, though much in his writing is very beautiful. I have read "Dombey and Son" since I have been here and liked it very much. "Ivanhoe" is among the best of the "Waverly Novels" though I like all that I have read very much.

I presume you will get perfect in the art of housekeeping, and I should like to get transported some morning to West Point, and get some of your buckwheat cakes and other good things. In a little less than five months more I will be a citizen again, and I presume I may remain so. Ex. Gov. Berry of N.H. who is a good friend to me is working a little get me a Lt's commission, but my position is such now it as a promotion I consider about out of the question, and I shall not reenlist in the V.R.C. Tell Mattie that I trust she will have just as good success as she desires. Please give my regards to all the folks at home and at the other houses.

Please write soon.
Very truly yours,
B. Cummings
Co.E 21st Reg. V.R.C.
Fort Wood N. Y. Harbor

In late June of 1864, General Jubal Early and his Confederate troops started to march toward Washington. By July 4 he had reached Harpers Ferry, and the people in Washington were near panic. All possible soldiers were rushed into place to defend the forts surrounding the Capitol, including regiments of the Veterans Reserve Corps. General Lew Wallace, the 23rd Wisconsin's commander in Cincinnati almost two years before, decided to intercept the Rebels with a small force in hopes the ensuing battle would delay them long enough for Grant to bring reinforcements to the defense of Washington. Although Wallace's troops were badly defeated on July 8, Grant did have time to bring in troops, and Early decided not to attack Washington. The firing Brainerd heard at Fort Stevens as reported in the following letter was not initiated by the Rebels to cover the retreat as he thought, but by the Union forces.

When Brainerd says he was the recipient of one of Gillmore's medals, he meant exactly that. The medal had been made on Gillmore's orders to be given to enlisted men who had distinguished themselves in the campaign in which Brainerd was wounded. It was a bronze medal with a picture of Fort Sumter on one side and the words, "For Gallant and Meritorious Conduct" on the other along with the general's autograph. Altogether there were 400 made.

Brainerd seems to have the name of Fort Sumter mixed up as he consistently calls it Fort Sumner. Charles Sumner was a radical Republican senator. There was also a Union general named Sumner who had two sons who were Union officers.

BRAINERD TO MARY:

Fort Slocum, Washington D.C. Aug 1st 1864

Friend Mary

Your very pleasant and very welcome letter of the date of July 29th was received last friday just as we were starting from Fort Sumner for this place, and I carried it in my pocket for some hours ere I had a chance to read it, and I read it in the evening in the quiet of the guard house when about all of the guard were asleep or on post, and myself as Cap. of the guard had nothing else to do for a few minutes.

I was carried by it right back to the time I was in West Point and to that first Sunday in your district when I had been twice disappointed in getting a boarding place, and I confess that I had some fear that I should be again when I applied to your father. I had noticed your house before and had twice passed it and wished that I might board there.

But though a boarder was not wanted, after it was decided to let me remain there was no disposition wanting to make me feel perfectly at home, and I always felt there as though I was in one of the most pleasant homes I ever had. Notwithstanding the anxieties and annoyance of teaching those were very pleasant times to me, and would have been still more so if I had been gifted with a more free, careless disposition, and more disposed to think people friendly and less fearful of pushing myself where I was not wanted. Had I taken it for granted that I was liked by all homes, and that my company was most always welcome, I think I should have got along more pleasantly and made more friends, though I might have sometimes been mistaken. But I preferred to err in the other direction if at all, and I was somewhat reserved with many and got the name of being as one girl expressed it "scornful" though I was far from that in feeling, yet there was a sort of savage independence about me which made me feel some indifference as to whether folks liked or disliked me outside of those that I was obliged to come in contact with and show more. But I did try to do my duty to my scholars and make them friends, how well I succeeded they must judge. I think I was treated as well as I deserved to be, and I have felt pretty sure that I made some friends.

Well I suppose you will wish to know how I happen to be here rather than at Fort Wood.

When the Rebs commenced their raid toward Washington Co. E. was ordered to report to Washington and friday July 8th we left Fort Wood, and the next night were in Washington. We remained there sunday until night when we marched out to Tennally town some three miles out of Georgetown and took up a position in the line of defences. We were then farely in the defences of Washington. Co.C. of the 21st with us and occupying Battery Rosell and we Co.E. the rifle pits to the left close to the Hd quarters of the 2nd Mass cavalry which did so much skirmishing during the raid (just been out to drill in light Artillery) where we remained until friday of that week and had rather a good time of it. To our left about a half a mile was Fort Reno and to our right Fort DeRussy[15] where there was some firing on the Rebs, and still farther on the right in the line of defence was Fort Stevens, the scene of the fight. You have read more of that than I can tell you. We could hear the skirmishing all of the time, and tuesday night rather expected an attack, but the attack on Fort Stevens was to cover the retreat. Wednesday the 6th Corp passed our position and we had the pleasure of seeing a large portion of it. The men were a war worn set certainly, the most so that I ever saw. Friday the two companies of the 21st went to the right into Fort DeRussy and Battery Smeade. Sunday we again moved to Cliffburne Barrack nearer Washington.

A week ago last friday our two companies were attached to the 7th VRC and again ordered out on the line of defences. This time we got into barracks at Forts Golten and Sumner, remained there a week and were again ordered to this fort and Fort Stevens, and the 7th Regt VRC and the two companies of the 21st for the garrison of those two forts. The location is not very pleasant nor very unpleasant. This fort is pretty much out of the way of every thing much more so than Fort Stevens. We are being used both as Infantry and as Heavy Artillery. I can content myself to remain here for eleven weeks after this when I hope to be a free man again and go on my way home rejoicing.

I wanted to visit Washington at the expense of U.S. and I have done so, and though I have been roughing it in comparison to what the fare was in New York I do not regret the change. I have been over the city some, visited the Capitol, Patent Office, Smithsonian Institute, and seen the other public buildings of the city but have not been into them. Washington is not a very attractive place to me and soldiers all dislike it and the vacinity. I shall not be an odd one.

I never suffered much mentally on account of my wounds, though the loss of my thumb and much of the use of my fore finger is going to be a great inconvenience almost to much to be very proud of. Still I would not have remained out of the service, and I have got off very well so far. Did I ever tell you that I was the recepient of one of Gillmore's medals? I have one in New York accompanied by a certificate from the Gen. It is a plain affair but rather acceptable on the whole. I remember Milton Bartholomew's daughter. She was quite pretty and gave promise of being more so in time. Please let me hear from once more at least while I am a soldier. Direct to Washington D.C. I hope to be in Andover Mass in twelve weeks and then I will write to you again if not before. Please give my regards to the folks at home and over to Isaac's, Mrs. Drew and the friends in West Point. My health is excellent.

I hope this letter will do you as much good as yours did me, though I can hardly hope it will. Gratefully your friend

B. Cummings
Co.E. 21st Regt.VRC
Washington D.C.

Brainerd Cummings's enlistment was up in October 1864, and he returned to Andover, Massachusetts. In the following letter it is quite clear that Brainerd has not been completely forthcoming with Mary concerning his possible marriage prospects.

BRAINERD TO MARY:

Andover Dec. 14th 1864

Dear Friends,

Owing to my absence from Andover your last letter did not reach me until some days after it got here, but it was very welcome when I did get it. And I hope it is not the last one that I shall get. I was happy to learn that the family was all well, and that Mattie had a good time on her visit North.

The army is such a drain on the young adult population that all kinds of laborers are in demand whether they are for the school-room or the farm. I almost wish I was not out of the line of teaching for carpenter work is rather cold winters. I was happy to hear so much from my acquaintances. I think Haynes Carter has done very well, much better than Ed. White. Henry Darnell has a right to be proud of his wife, and if she is as pretty woman as she was girl I do not see how he can well help it. Lysander and wife are getting a head first; Mell is letting them go it while they are young. Please excuse that slang phrase.

Dave and Ed Richmond have pretty good positions. I feel very much like getting back into the army again at times and would do so if I could get a good position. However I do not expect much to go into the army again. Since I have been in Andover I have been at work at my trade most of the time while in town and presume I may remain here this winter, but it is uncertain.

Well, Mary, the confirmed old Bach as you professed to think has at last been and gone and done it, and is now a bachelor no more. Tuesday evening, Nov. 22nd a Miss Sarah H. Holt, and your humble servant called on the minister and in a very short space of time were made one, as the saying is. The thing was done very quietly being witnessed by only a few friends and was a couple of days sooner than curious friends were looking for it. The next morning we started for Maine, and at night appeared to my sisters very much to their surprise and I think very much to their gratification. We spent about ten days among friends there very pleasantly, and a week ago last Monday returned to Andover and we are now domiciled with her mother.

It is quite a change from army life and rations to liveing a citizen and boarding with Mrs. Brainerd Cummings. However the change is decidedly pleasant. She says I may give her love to any of my old friends and so I send a portion to you. When you will send us that photograph we will try to send you ours. I hope that you will not entirely forget me now that I am out of the army and married.

I assure you that I should be very glad to hear from you at any and all times you can make it convenient to let me. I was not in a hurry to get married, but rather thought always I should do it when I got ready and I did. Think I have made out about as well in that line as my Lodi acquaintences. Please give my regards to all the folks at home and to Isaac's.

Please let us hear from you soon. I take none the less interest in old friends for being married.

Very truly yours,
B. Cummings

This is the last existing letter from Brainerd Cummings. He mentioned Ed's reenlistment but said nothing about the ring Ed gave to Mary. If she had told Brainerd about it, he surely would have said something.

In January of 1865 Brainerd Cummings applied for a disability pension stating that his right arm was "struck by a musket ball which passed through the arm injuring the cords badly and then passed into his right side cutting the muscles four inches in length and the skin is now grown fast to the ribs, that his arm in painful at times and is rendered weak so that he cannot hard work with it."

Since he had been transferred from Co. A, 7th Regiment, New Hampshire Volunteers, to Co. E, 21st Reg. VRC, he had a hard time proving that he was indeed discharged from the army, but he finally received a pension of $17.00 a month. He died of cancer in Andover on December 10, 1900, just eighteen days after his thirty-sixth wedding anniversary. Sarah died ten years later. They had no children.

ENDNOTES

1. John D. Billings, *Hardtack and Coffee: The Unwritten Story of Army Life* (1887; reprint, Lincoln: University of Nebraska Press, 1993), 113.
2. Ibid., 46-48.
3. Shelby Foote, *The Civil War, Fort Sumter to Perryville*, vol. 1 (New York: Random House, 1958; Vintage Books, 1991), 729.
4. Ibid., 739.
5. The letters from Brainerd Cummings to Mary Van Ness are given in the Appendix.
6. Foote, *The Civil War, Fort Sumter to Perryville*, vol. 1, 709.
7. This information was taken from Ed Richmond's post-war application for a military pension. A copy of the application was found with Ed's letters.
8. Mark M. Boatner III, *The Civil War Dictionary* (New York: Random House, 1988; Vintage Books, 1991), 119-121.
9. This and other regimental information was taken from *A Compendium of the War of the Rebellion* by Frederick H. Dyer and the *Official Army Register of the Volunteer Force of the U.S. Army for the Years 1861-1865*, vol. 3.
10. See the letters of Brainerd Cummings in the Appendix.
11. A philipena gift was given by the loser to the winner in a game popular at the time. For further details see *Oxford English Dictionary*, vol. 7 (Oxford: Oxford University Press, 1933), 775.
12. Sewing is the best I can transcribe this word although a sewing circle seems an odd activity for a man. [Susan T. Puck]
13. Handwriting or penmanship.
14. Boatner, *The Civil War Dictionary*, 870.
15. There were two forts named Fort De Russy. The better known one was a Confederate fort in Louisiana captured by U.S. troops in March 1864.

Bibliographical Note

The letters have all been transcribed from the originals in my possession except for the two previously mentioned. The information on the soldiers' lives after the war came from their Military and Pension Records in the National Archives except for Edgar Richmond's, which came from family records. Regimental information was from *A Compendium of the War of the Rebellion* by Frederick H. Dyer and the *Official Army Register of the Volunteer Force of the U.S. Army for the Years 1861–1865,* Vol. III. Other information on individuals came from public records. I tried where possible to verify the family records independently but was not always able to do so.

Many sources were consulted for general history. Chief among these was Shelby Foote's monumental three volume *The Civil War, A Narrative.* Others were *The Civil War Day by Day* edited by John S. Bowman, *The Civil War Sourcebook, A Traveler's Guide* by Chuck Lawless, *The Civil War Dictionary* by Mark Boatner III, *American Heritage's Picture History of the Civil War* by Bruce Caton, and *The Atlas to Accompany the Official Records of the Union and Confederate Armies.* For the everyday details of Army life, *Hardtack and Coffee* by John D. Billings was invaluable. Written by a veteran twenty or so years after the war and recently released in paperback, it is full of detail and delightfully written.

The history is as accurate as I can make it. The places where I have made suppositions or conjectures are clearly stated and are based upon the evidence in either the letters or other original material. While I have some other speculations about certain relationships and events, I did not include them as the evidence does not clearly support them.

I would like to thank The Bancroft Library for the copies of the official maps and James P. Schmeidlin of Lodi, Wisconsin, for the picture of Will Shurtleff. I also owe a huge debt to my children, my son-in-law, my sister, Patricia Barnes, and my friends Jean Frank Mulford and William J. Baker for their help and encouragement, and to my grandson Will Iverson for dragging me, kicking and screaming, into the computer age.

Susan T. Puck

Index